So...What *Are* You Doing After College?

So...What *Are* You Doing After College?

Real-Life Advice

from People

Who've Been There

Edited by Sven Newman

AN OWL BOOK

HENRY HOLT AND COMPANY • NEW YORK

Henry Holt and Company, Inc.
Publishers since 1866
115 West 18th Street
New York, New York 10011

Henry Holt® is a registered
trademark of Henry Holt and Company, Inc.

Published in Canada by Fitzhenry & Whiteside Ltd.,
195 Allstate Parkway, Markham, Ontario L3R 4T8.

Library of Congress Cataloging-in-Publication Data

So . . . what *are* you doing after college? : real-life advice from
people who've been there / edited by Sven Newman.
p.   cm.
"An Owl Book."
Includes bibliographical references.
1. Vocational guidance—United States.   2. College graduates—
Employment—United States.   3. Degrees, Academic—
United States.
I. Newman, Sven.
HF5382.5.U5S565   1995   95-19934
331.7'02—dc20   CIP

ISBN 0-8050-3467-6

Henry Holt books are available for special promotions
and premiums. For details contact:
Director, Special Markets.

First Edition—1995

Designed by Jessica Shatan

Printed in the United States of America
All first editions are printed on acid-free paper.∞

10   9   8   7   6   5   4   3   2   1

Contents

Acknowledgments

My utmost gratitude to Kirsten Lee Soares. Without her encouragement and thoughtful comments, this book would never have been what it is today. My thanks to John Javna for teaching me the trade and to Tracy Sherrod for believing in an idea and making it better. My gratitude to all the people who've selflessly offered help along the way—Dave Geary, Michael Huttner, Lenna Lebovitch, Sharolyn Hovlind, Christine Miller, and Christine Chin, among others. Thank you to my family and housemates for their support. And, most important, my appreciation and admiration goes out to the writers, whose stories and words are what make this book worth reading.

Introduction

About a year after I graduated from college I was finally able to look back with a little humor at the state of panic I had worked myself into worrying about what I would do after college. Reminiscing with friends over a couple of bottles of wine, I found it was easy to chuckle at the angst we'd all experienced back in college contemplating our fate in the "real world." But while we were going through this soul-searching process, it wasn't so comical. After sixteen years of school, we had all grown comfortable with the set goals and defined directions of academia and, frankly, to be confronted with the reality that no one was telling us what to do next was a little daunting. Sure, it was great that the whole world was open to us—in some sense that was exactly what we wanted—but having that liberty was also overwhelming and, at times, even miserable. To make matters worse, everyone and their cousin seemed to take an interest in our post-graduation plans. "So . . . ," their interrogations would always begin, followed by that dreaded query, "What *are* you doing after college?"

It was a good question, and one we all wanted to have an answer to, but making a decision was hard with such limited information about what was really out there. It's true that the career center was brimming with job listings, graduate school pamphlets, corporate brochures, and other postcollege paraphernalia, but nothing gave us the candid details we craved. What we really wanted was to be able to look into the future and see what we might experience were we to choose a particular path. We wanted to know what it would feel like to be an entry-level employee running around an ad agency; a Teach For America instructor standing in front of an inner-city class; a graduate student sitting in a library two years after everyone else has been out in the working world, a backpacking traveler perched atop some Tibetan mountain peak; a freelance writer trying to pay the rent; and so many other things.

It was that yearning for real-life information that inspired this book. As the wine was passed around at our casual gathering, we shared our collective knowledge about life after college. I listened to friends recount stories of what they had envisioned the post-college world to be and what they had actually found after they stepped off the graduation stage: Kelly described what her life was like working at a shelter for troubled children; Helen talked excitedly about being an intern for a public television station; Andrew had tales to tell about the tribulations of working in sales at an insurance company; Sabrina offered her perspective on life in the advertising world. Sitting there, hearing straightforward talk about the emotional challenges of counseling heat-packing kids and HIV-positive teens, the rewards of documentary film editing, and the frustrations of trying to succeed in sales, I realized I was listening to the real experts on life after college. These recent graduates were the resource I had wanted to hear from when I was trying to make my decision.

The next day, as I sat at my desk at a small environmental publishing firm where I had found my niche after graduation, the idea began to gel. If I could track down recent graduates who had gone in different directions and ask them to share some of their thoughts about the postcollege paths they had taken, their combined stories could be helpful for others trying to make decisions about life after college.

That's what this book is all about.

It's meant to be casual. It's supposed to be candid. Hopefully, it's a little like sitting down with a group of friends and a bottle of wine and listening to their tales about what it's like to be laboring late nights on Wall Street; working your way through Europe as a grape picker; struggling with idealism and political reality while working as a White House intern; making it on peanuts as a novice screenplay writer; and living out many other intriguing postcollege paths.

When you're in a pre-graduation panic it's not always easy to believe, but there are many fulfilling ways to spend your time after college. These essays are proof. The people who have shared their stories here were only recently confused graduates-to-be themselves, yet they have uncovered a wide range of meaningful and rewarding opportunities. There's Steve de Brun, who decided to bicycle from California to Chile, and Kim Green, a woman who wasn't sure she fit in to the working world, but found that her passion for music made her perfect for a job at Sony Records. Then there's Sayantani DasGupta, who writes about what it's like to be a late-blooming medical student; Roger Bearden, who shares the rewards he's discovered teaching English in Eastern Europe; Amy Dalton, who discusses the opportunities she's found in small business, and so many others, each describing another possibility for life after graduation.

So . . . what are *you* going to do after college? You could work for a television news program, write for a newspaper, join an advertising agency, or save up some money and take a lap around the globe. Perhaps you will become a management consultant or an English teacher in Japan. Maybe you'll join the Peace Corps. And hopefully the candid tales these recent graduates have written will help you get there.

Getting Creative

Ask people to name a typical postcollege job and chances are they will come up with some sort of business position—being a sales rep for a big-name corporation, working for a bank, or maybe doing marketing for a small start-up company. But the funny thing is that there are so many overlooked alternatives. As you are reading this, there are college graduates who are out there being paid to design CD covers and Internet home pages, write magazine articles about suntan lotion and solar eclipses, take photographs of bicycle tourists and hold newsroom cue cards, and pick out film locations and review movie scripts. These kinds of creative alternatives are just as much a part of the postcollege job world as conventional business career positions. And if you are an art history major who prefers paints to pinstripes, an English major with a predilection for prose, or maybe just someone who enjoys being around creative-minded people, these kinds of jobs might be worth exploring.

What you'll find on the following pages are stories written by like-minded graduates describing the creative opportunities they uncovered after school. These graduates are writers and musicians, filmmakers and media hounds. Some of them knew exactly what they wanted when they graduated. Plenty had no idea. What's heartening is they've all found ways to do the creative work they enjoy.

Hopefully some of their thoughts and stories may inspire your own search. The options these graduates have written about barely scratch the surface of the wide-ranging possibilities for creative-minded people, but they can provide ideas. In addition, these graduates' tales reveal a great deal about the process of getting to that ideal creative position, whatever it may be. While some graduates luck out and fall into their dream job right away, many others arrive through a series of steps. Some start out performing administrative tasks at a creative company just to get their foot in the door. Others opt for unpaid internships, moonlighting to pay the rent. Some find freelancing to be a way to make inroads, and others still begin by serving as assistants to more established professionals.

As you begin to explore your options, it may be worthwhile to remember how these little steps may pay off in the long run. If writing is your passion, taking a stab at an article for a local publication may be the path to finding a paid job later on. If you're interested in photography, working as a photographer's assistant may be the perfect way to pick up skills. Volunteering on a movie set may give you the experience and contacts to secure a real job on another film. Doing freelance work, serving as an assistant, even working for free can get you closer to where you want to go. At least that's what these graduates found. In the end, their essays are about creative people who believed it was possible to find post-college opportunities that would allow them to utilize their talents and worked at it until they found a way to get there.

Finding a Fit

in the Music

Industry

Kim Green

Let's be honest, most graduates-to-be don't know exactly what they want to do after college. Once out in the working world, they drift toward their interests and, hopefully, find a niche where they are happy. Here's an encouraging story of a woman who wasn't sure she would fit in at all but has found a perfect place for her eccentricities in the entertainment industry.

First let me introduce myself. I am an African-American woman. I have six earrings in my right ear and three in my left. I have four tattoos (three of which are visible at any given time). They are all music symbols. There's an eighth note, a treble clef, the melody of my favorite song tattooed around my ankle, and a harp that adorns my forearm. These tattoos represent me. They are a "written" testimony that music is the most important thing to me. What do the earrings mean? I just like them.

My parents weren't the only people who used to worry that I'd never get a job looking like this. I worried, too. Forget the tattoos, I can't even get up in the morning and I hate stockings, dresses, and high-heeled pumps. As my senior year of college approached,

I was more nervous than most. I had two concerns: Am I gonna get a job? and What kind of job could a person like me get?

Not everyone fits into the mold that college prepares us for. But I am a living example that everyone and anyone can find a job that they want (and that wants them). The key is being courageous enough to be yourself. By being honest with myself about the fact that I was not the "average" graduate, I knew that the job search would not be smooth, but I stayed as true to myself as possible and plunged in.

I knew I wanted to work in the music industry, although none of my studies reflected that. Only my record collection and my heart. But I was determined and told everyone who asked me. I thought that by putting it into the "universe," someone might hear me. At the time it seemed absurd. I was sure the only way to get in was to know someone, and I knew no one. But I gave myself a kick in the butt and started doing some freelance writing for small music magazines (for little or no money). I didn't know how that would help, but I thought I'd better start doing something musical.

Thus began a long path of work experiences that paved the way for me to land on the doorstep of the job that is perfect for me. And, I might add, I am perfect for it!

As a copywriter at Sony Music, my immense and profound love of music, my journalistic ability, and my expertise in advertising are simultaneously put to work. My job requires me to know and connect with all kinds of music (which comes naturally) and write catchy, concise, and memorable ad copy. But even more important, I am selling something I believe in. Sometimes it's difficult because real issues come up, forcing me to weigh my morals, my good humor, and my genuine appreciation for art. Do we or do we not put guns in an ad, even if the name of the album is *In Guns We Trust*? Do I want to use the word *nigger* in an ad that thousands of young black children will read, even if that word is throughout the song? (The answer is no, by the way.) Powerful stuff.

THE JOURNEY

How did I get here? A lot of faith, determination, and a willingness to go the long route. I have had six jobs since I've been out of college, not including my recurring job at Tower Records every summer vacation. And I did not go by the trite and unrealistic "rule" that said I should stay at least one year at each job so that my résumé would indicate stability. I did, however, create a rule for myself: take any job that will teach you something.

My first job was at Macy's. I was recruited straight off campus and brought in as a junior executive trainee. Although writing headlines like "Ceiling Fans Only $99.99!" was not exactly what I called creative advertising, Macy's was a great place to learn what it was like to work in an actual art department and to work closely with art directors. I learned about graphics, computerized layouts, typefaces, font sizes, and the crucial difference between a comp, a layout, and a mechanical. I also learned that I didn't want to write about products I had never seen or touched.

Although I had studied advertising for four years, the thought of package advertising suddenly seemed like a scam to me. It was lying, and I knew I could never be good at it. Major setback. I had earned a degree in advertising and hated it.

When I was offered a nonwriting job at the Bantam Doubleday Dell Publishing Group as an administrative assistant to a national accounts manager, I worried that I wouldn't be writing, but I needed the time to step back and see if I even really wanted to write. The national accounts manager's job was to sell books to wholesalers. My job was to prepare him to go out on his sales calls each month. The position required meticulous administrative abilities.

I added another task: watch the executive-assistant relationship closely. I observed important things, such as in the time it took him to explain how I should return a certain phone call, he could have done it himself. There I learned how to be a good assistant as well as how to treat one. More important, I learned that I needed to be writing again.

For my next job I worked at a direct marketing advertising

agency. I know I thought advertising wasn't for me, but this was a great opportunity, and I had a degree in it! As the only copywriter on staff, I figured I'd get the recognition I needed, gather a body of work for my portfolio, and gain the confidence to eventually be able to write what I wanted. I was responsible for a multitude of products, from All-state Legal Supplies to the Betty Crocker catalog. I wrote blurbs of copy for everything from legal forms to bunny-shaped muffin pans. The company was tiny, the work load was heavy, and the pressure was on. The job taught me to care enough about this discipline of "writing copy" to form opinions about it. I saw that having an opinion garnered respect, if nothing else. And it taught me that agency work is not for me. Eventually the ultimate truth surfaced: if you don't care about what you're writing, it shows. The small agency and the Betty Crocker pans began to wear thin, and my obvious apathy was starting to show. I was willing to leave writing again to move out of advertising once and for all.

GETTING WARMER

I was lucky enough to land a job as the assistant to the producer of the Benson and Hedges Blues Festival at Festival Productions. Although it was a grueling two months (yes, only two months), I felt like I had arrived. This was the music industry. I could wear what I wanted, tattoos, earrings, and all! Although there were a lot of personalities to deal with, everyone was measured by their effectiveness, not their personal style. I felt comfortable. I could be free. I could be myself and work hard. It was love. Work didn't end at five o'clock. There was work on weekends, but there was also gratification. Putting together a concert series and watching it unfold was amazing. Taking calls from people all over the country who were begging for tickets to our show made me feel that what we had worked so hard to create was ready for consumption and the people wanted it. I was also grateful to be near artists. I could relate. I remember one day one of us forgot to carry B. B. King's guitar, Lucille. He was very upset. We never forgot again. I learned to respect the mind of the artist. That experience showed me that music was where I belonged, though not exactly producing concerts.

Two months there and on to my next job: the New York City Transit Authority. Writing again. I was offered what seemed an enormous salary at the time to work in the Corporate Communications Department. I was the associate editor of the Transit Authority newsletter. Since there are forty thousand employees, it is a substantial paper. Immediately, however, I knew it was too corporate, too male-dominated, and too boring. But I learned the art of writing corporate prose. I also learned that I had to get out of there.

The Perfect Fit

Then, finally, I landed my job at Sony Music as a copywriter. It came after I successfully completed three freelance assignments writing advertisements for them. I couldn't believe it, it was a job that seemed tailored for me and I got it because I'm me! My boss loved the fact that I love harpist Andreas Vollenweider as much as I love LL Cool J.

Tears came to my eyes the first day I entered my new office in the CBS "Black Rock" building in New York. It was equipped with mounted speakers and a beautiful new stereo. I looked around and knew all my previous drudgery jobs had not been in vain. My job here uses all of my skills. Because I am responsible for over fifty artists, my administrative and organizational skills come in handy. Working at the small agency taught me the importance of client relationships. And even though Sony's ad department is "in-house," our clients are the Columbia and Epic labels. Often they can be as demanding if not more so than if we were an outside agency.

Because of the way the advertising department is structured (and the work load is so outrageous), each copywriter is a miniagency unto him- or herself. We're each responsible for taking directions from the product manager, getting proper due dates from traffic,

and coming up with and executing a concept. We each have a genre of music that we "specialize in" (read *love*) and a roster of artists for whom we're responsible.

My days are fun. Some of them are spent listening to music, "getting a vibe" and just seeing what the music feels like. If it's a new artist, I have to wonder, What are they trying to say with this album? (especially if it's called *In Guns We Trust*) and What about it appeals to the consumer? The music? The lyrics? The politics? If I'm working with a more experienced artist, I have to ask, What are they saying that's different than before? How have they changed? Is this album for their old fans or are they looking for new fans?

Then I look at my "work request" and see if it's an ad for a trade magazine or a consumer magazine. Then I figure out the most effective (and inoffensive) ways of convincing radio stations to play it, retailers to stock it, and consumers to consume it. That is my job in a nutshell.

Some of the other elements involve communicating with the higher-ups about my ideas, making changes when the client doesn't like them, and fighting for my ideas when they should like them. Another part of my job has been to introduce the idea of the black marketplace and its needs to a company that has only recently quadrupled its black music roster and is still in what I call "urban shock." My job is often to be the voice and the mind of the black consumer and artist, and to create advertising that is honest yet responsible. My job is to write about music, care about music, and make sure others do, too. My job is . . . to be me.

What does this mean?

Well, after reading Studs Terkel's *Working* (read it!), I realized that working is all-encompassing. It ties in to who we are in the world and what our purpose is. In that book, waiters and waitresses spoke of their jobs as art and doctors and lawyers mumbled about how bored they were.

I realized that whatever I was going to do, it had to be something that touched me as much as I touched it. It had to be something that meant something to me. And it had to be something that I was great at because of who I am as a person, not because of the credentials on my wall. By being determined to find that job, I found it, despite fears that I'd never settle down. I spend most of my time working, and I do it well, because I care about this work. I was often frustrated by the idea that I'd have to work for the rest of my life. At times I resigned myself to the fact that I'd never be happy—I was too weird and too resistant to structure.

But as I always say, the entertainment industry is a safe haven for people who just don't fit. And by the size of it, I see, I am not all alone. You won't be either.

Some Advice from Kim

Being a Music Journalist: If you want to be a music journalist, write for *free*. What you need most are clips of your work. Pick up free newspapers in your neighborhood or hometown and write a letter to the editor. Send an idea for an article to local magazines. (If the magazine does pay a small amount, but the editor seems skeptical about your skills or idea, offer to do it for free.)

Get a Business Card: It's a neat and tidy way of having your number readily and legibly available. You can have a card made inexpensively but tastefully. Have no fear about giving yourself a title: "writer," "production assistant," "administrative assistant," "organizer."

Be Flexible: Don't turn down that administrative assistant job at a record company, even if you used to be a store *manager*. It's not a step down, it's a step in. If you can't find any position in a record company, there are a million other ways in. With the information superhighway coming our way, even computers are becoming an integral part of the music industry. Production, video, film, makeup artistry, hair styling, even catering—all of these areas touch the music industry, and you will find yourself constantly meeting the people you need to know to get where you're going.

Be Patient: The music industry is not going anywhere. It is constantly changing and moving in and out of trends. Therefore, there are certain areas that are like a revolving door, meaning there is always a way in for you—for example, publicity, promotion, artists and repertoire. If you feel you've been pushing hard for one thing and still can't get in, go do and learn something else for a while. You'll come back with a new perspective and more great work experience under your belt.

Be Social: "Music heads," as I call them, love to go out and be seen. They are always in nightclubs, in restaurants, and at parties. Go to these places as much as possible. Not only is it fun, it gives you a firsthand look at what type of songs the crowd dances to and what kind of songs prompt them to walk off the dance floor. You can see the differences between rock clubs and rap clubs, catch the cultural trends, notice what kind of crowd smokes more than they drink, and so on. These are actually the kinds of things you will discuss when coming up with innovative ways to market music.

Be Visible: The music industry is extremely image conscious. Make your appearance memorable. Look stylish and look distinctive. Make sure the people "on the scene" remember who you are. My tattoos did wonders for me!

Know Your Popular Icons: Listen to all kinds of music, see all kinds of movies, and read *Entertainment Weekly*. It is the Cliff Notes of the entertainment field. It's a fast read and has an insightful way of looking at the trends, contradictions, and indications of the industry. It will give you tons of conversational ammunition, and as you read it more and more, you will find which aspect of the industry you are most drawn to.

A Few Resources to Help You Out

Rhythm and Blues: A Life in American Music, by Jerry Wexler and David Ritz (New York: St. Martin's Press, 1994). A highly acclaimed memoir of one of the industry's great producers. This book provides a juicy, anecdotal history of the music world.

Hit Men: Power Brokers and Fast Money Inside the Music Business, by Frederic Dannen (New York: Vintage Books/Random House, 1991). "A sobering, blunt and unusually well-observed depiction of the sometimes sordid inner workings of the music business," says *Billboard* magazine.

Networking in the Music Industry: Making the Contacts You Need to Succeed in the Music Business, by Jim Clevo and Eric Olsen (San Diego: Rockpress Publishing, 1993). A compilation of interviews with more than a hundred music industry professionals. Written both for aspiring musicians and those looking to get into the industry side of things.

The Death of Rhythm and Blues, by Nelson George (New York: Pantheon/Random House, 1987). This book provides a wonderful history of how the various musical genres have evolved.

The Life of
a Reporter

Stephen Kim

Writing for a newspaper is much more than a nine-to-five desk job. As Stephen discovered during his one-year internship in journalism, being a cub reporter is as much an education in human nature as it is an entry-level job. In this essay he highlights some of the challenges he confronted and lessons he learned during his stint in the newsroom.

Mrs. Pitts was a small, timid-looking woman. It was hard for me to imagine the scene at her home only hours before. Billy, her shy fifteen-year-old son, had already left for school when Mr. Pitts pulled into the driveway after a trip to the pharmacy. He climbed down from the cab of his pickup, but he never made it to the house. A single shotgun blast knocked him down onto the rocky walkway fifteen feet in front of the house. The shot pellets left a neat circular pattern of blood on his chest, killing him instantly. He died clutching his house keys in one hand and a pharmacy bag in the other.

Mrs. Pitts dialed 911 and told the operator to send help immediately. She had just shot her husband.

When police arrived on the scene, Mrs. Pitts refused to talk. As police placed her in custody that day, Mrs. Pitts maintained a strict silence, refusing to say anything about that morning's events or her relationship with her husband.

Now Mrs. Pitts clutched a tattered Kleenex in one hand and was sobbing softly as she took a seat next to me in a spare office in the jail. I thanked her for meeting with me and asked if she could describe what had happened that morning.

Her response was a stern *no*.

"The only reason I agreed to speak with you," she informed me, "was to make sure Billy was OK."

I assured her I would look into her son's care and then asked again if she could tell me anything about the events of that morning. Over and over she responded that she had nothing else to say.

After twenty minutes of stonewalling, I was ready to close my notebook and give up. I asked her one last time, "Are you sure you have nothing to say about your husband's death?"

She took a deep breath and then gave me one terse statement: "All I can say is I didn't want to shoot him, and can't believe I did it."

My hand shook as I frantically scribbled her words into my notebook. Here I was, twenty-one years old, less than six months out of college with barely a lick of experience, and I had stumbled onto a shocking homicide and the chilling confession of a frightened young woman.

My encounter with Mrs. Pitts is one of many memorable examples of the random, sometimes bizarre, and certainly rewarding experiences I've encountered as a cub newspaper reporter. Besides taking jailhouse confessions, I've found myself leaning over the side of a rowboat off the Connecticut shore, trying to interview an environmentalist swimming across the Long Island Sound; wading ankle-deep in raw sewage while covering an industrial park accident; and wringing out my soaked notebook during an interview next to the dolphin tank at a local amusement park.

THE BEAT

In the abstract, the simplest way to describe the job of a journalist is to say we tell stories. The journalist's everyday responsibility is

to take a story, research it, and then condense and weave the resulting glut of information into a readable account. In practical terms, being a journalist means you can stick your nose into lots of places and then tell people about it.

Exactly what stories and places you will encounter depends partly on what kind of newspaper you find yourself working for. If you are starting out at a small-town weekly paper, you'll be covering the whole spectrum of local news, everything from town meetings to the county fair and the local high school football games.

If you're starting out at a daily paper, you might end up with the night cops beat listening to the police radio channels, which was my first job at the *Fort Worth Star-Telegram* in Arlington, Texas. Every day I'd check into the office at 3 P.M. and park myself in front of the police scanner to sip my coffee and bide my time. Whenever anything interesting came up—traffic accidents, fires, or any other misadventure—I'd grab my notebook and jump in the car. On a good day I might cover a three-alarm apartment fire, or good day I might cover all three. By the end of the night, I would have interviewed two dozen people, pleaded with emergency room personnel for patient information, waited anxiously for a police sergeant to return my call, and filed all three stories for the morning paper. This beat can be intense and exhausting, but it's also an incredible experience.

What You Get Out of It

Journalism is about writing, and there's no doubt that doing a stint as a cub reporter will hone your skills as a writer. Like any college student, I'd written my share of assigned papers and had even done some writing for my college paper, but nothing compared to what I learned on the job. Daily deadline story pressure under the critical eye of an editor is bound to improve your speed and clarity. In addition to learning to distill pages of quotes and facts into a fifteen-inch one-column story, a reporter must exercise a great deal of creativity within that allotted space to grab the reader's attention, spin a tale, *and* make it real to the audience. Who do I contact first? How much should I reveal to this source? How do I resolve the inconsistency between competing accounts of an event or issue? All of these tactical questions are woven into the task, making your writing that much more of a challenge and a learning experience.

Reporting is also a crash course in human nature. I can think of no other job that would have allowed me to come into contact with so many people or situations right out of college. In the span of a single week, a reporting job has taken me from the warm, plush interior of the mayor's office to the filthy rooms of a crack house. My job has been to pry inside the lives of attorneys, juvenile delinquents, grieving families, disappointed political candidates, animal rights activists, and an occasional celebrity.

One of the greatest joys I've found in this job is getting to know folks who, although ordinary on the outside, are quite remarkable in every other respect. Take Sherry Close, a single mother of five (including twins) living off food stamps and child support, whom I was assigned to profile. Facing a desperate future, Close decided to take control of her life and beat the odds: she enrolled in classes at a local community college. Five years later, she graduated from the University of Texas at Arlington with a degree in electrical engineering and landed a job with a local firm. "Everybody was telling me I can't do it," Close told me during the first of several interviews. "I guess that made me more determined than ever." The story of this incredible woman made page one and elicited a tremendous response, even including a letter from then President Bush, honoring Close for her extraordinary efforts. Sometimes being a reporter means sitting back, saying "Wow!" and letting a good story tell itself.

Of course, like every job, journalism has its downside. Financially, beginning reporters don't make nearly what they deserve. As a general rule, on payday, I avoided calling my friends working in corporate America. Although there was never any doubt in my mind that my job was far more interesting than what any of my friends were doing, it was still difficult to overlook the fact that they were making twice my salary.

Reporting can also take its toll on you mentally and physically. People who refuse to talk or return phone calls when your deadline is mere hours away certainly put stress in your day. Dashing out in the middle of the night to chase cops and ambulances makes it worse.

As with any entry-level position, being a cub reporter also means performing tedious tasks. When you're starting out, you always have to do more than your fair share of mundane assignments. For every front-page article there are dozens of stories about tonight's Kiwanis Club meeting or tomorrow's zoning board agenda that will be buried in the back of the paper. Even though your relatives are about the only ones who will ever read these articles, you still have to slog through the research, make the phone calls, attend the meetings, and write the stories.

But in spite of the negatives, I can honestly say my choice to plunge into journalism after graduation has been the best decision of my life so far. If you're naturally curious, a little bit adventurous, and willing to take on a demanding but extremely rewarding job, consider this: someone may be willing to pay you to meet news makers, witness dramatic events, and chronicle it all for thousands of readers. For me, journalism has been fulfilling for a variety of reasons, but most importantly because it's been fun.

Some Advice from Stephen

Where to Look for a Job: The local papers in the area around your college and in the area where you grew up are two of the best places to look for work. In both places you have an advantage because you've lived in the community. Knowing the area gives you a lot more credibility than someone from outside.

Interviews: Wherever you land an interview, make sure you know the local news before you go in. Know the mayor, know the local issues, and definitely know what's in that day's paper! During one interview, I had someone ask my opinion about an article in the paper, which I hadn't read, and as a result, the interview was a disaster.

Clippings: To find a job in journalism, you really need clippings of articles you've written. I don't think there is anyplace that will give you a job without them. The easiest way to get a couple of articles is through school: the daily paper, a weekly journal—whatever publications are available. If you're lucky you might even be able to find a local paper that will hire you as a stringer for local high school sports.

Job Fairs: Ask at your career center about journalism job fairs. There are a number of different fairs put on by various organizations—the Asian-American Journalists Association, the National Association of Black Journalists, regional journalism associations, and so forth—that will have leads for both entry-level positions and internships.

Assignments: As much as you can, try to show enthusiasm and put effort into every project you're assigned. Starting out, you're going to be stuck with the mundane stories, but the only way to get better assignments is to develop a good track record. The only way to do this is to throw yourself into the projects you're assigned, no matter how trivial they may seem.

Taking Initiative: Writing is really only half of reporting. The other half is making sure you are covering your beat well. While most of the work you will do will probably be stories that are assigned to you, there's nothing wrong with showing initiative and coming up with your own leads.

Getting Criticism: It's very important to seek out feedback on your writing from your editors and from other reporters. A lot of writers don't do that because it's intimidating. You don't really want to hear all that's wrong with your writing, but really, it's the best way to improve.

A Few Resources to Help You Out

Columbia Journalism Review (Graduate School of Journalism, Columbia University, New York, N.Y. 10027, [212] 854-2716). Bimonthly trade journal that provides insight into the industry. It also contains a classified section with job listings. Look for it in your college library.

Asian-American Journalists Association (1765 Sutter Street, Room 1000, San Francisco, Calif. 94115, [415] 346-2051). This organization offers a mentor program, scholarships, career advice, a twenty-four-hour job hotline, and an annual job fair. To find out about local chapters, call the national office.

National Association of Black Journalists (11600 Sunrise Valley Drive, Reston, Va. 22091, [703] 648-1270). Students can join for twenty dollars. Benefits include a twenty-four-hour job hotline, an annual job fair, and a monthly publication covering what members in the industry are doing. Call for more information and to find out about local chapters.

National Association of Hispanic Journalists (National Press Building, Suite 1193, Washington, D.C. 20045, [202] 662-7145). This association provides scholarships, seminars, workshops, and job placement assistance.

Working as a
Production
Assistant in
Broadcast News

Samantha Sherman

Crazy hours, pressure to perform, and plenty of entry-level tasks—it's all a part of starting out in television news. It's not for everyone, but some people, like Samantha, thrive on it.

During my senior year, the thought of life after college gave me the creeps. Actually, it was more like asthma. I'd break into a cold sweat, get hot flashes (if it's possible to suffer from both symptoms at the same time), and start hyperventilating. I'd try breathing deeply, but it never helped. Sometimes I'd pat my pockets, feeling for cigarettes, and I don't even smoke. It was a nightmare, and one I couldn't shake, no matter how hard I tried.

I knew I didn't want to go back to school, had neither the talent nor the inclination to go the traditional corporate route, and was too scared to blow my savings traveling. I needed a job, but none of the companies recruiting at my school interested me. Finally I sat down and thought about what I liked to do. I loved discussing current events. In fact, when I look back at my childhood, it seems like that's all my family ever did. So when someone suggested broadcast news, it sounded like a good idea—you cover a variety of topics, so it never gets boring; you try to answer important questions, so it's intellectual; you educate the public about relevant social issues, so you can think of it as a form of community service; and if you're lucky, someday you might make a lot of money and become a minor celebrity. I applied for an internship at one of the network affiliates near my college town, got it, liked it, and was offered a job when it ended. Fairy-tale story, right?

Well, partly. It sounds incredible for an entry-level job that requires only a bachelor of arts, and it is. But of course there are negatives as well. Being a production assistant also means being underpaid and underappreciated. In other words, you're at the bottom of the totem pole. Anytime anyone needs anything done— a fact checked, a phone call made, a map found—it is usually dumped on the PA. It's kind of like being a student. Your work is never done; you just stop when you feel you've put in enough hours and it's late.

What Does a Production Assistant Do?

On top of being everyone's personal gopher, PAs have a number of regular duties, such as maintaining the tape library. Whenever a reporter wants a clip of anything the station has ever aired, you're the one who gets to find it. Some days it takes two seconds. Other days you spend forty-five minutes scanning the database for a tape, pulling it, rewinding it, just to have the reporter decide it's not what he or she wants after all. PAs also operate the TelePrompTer— the system that superimposes the anchor's script directly into the face of the camera. In case this breaks down, PAs also make sure everyone has a hard copy of the text. When scripts are printed minutes or seconds before airtime, it can mean frantic paper sorting, mad dashes down the halls, and countless paper cuts. And on a meager PA's salary, Band-Aids don't come cheap. PAs are also responsible for Chyrons. That's the writing the viewer sees on the TV screen, such as sports scores, the anchor's name, or the credits at the end of the show.

THE EARLY SHIFT

When you start out, there's a good chance you won't work during normal daylight hours. You won't put in eighty- or ninety-hour weeks, but you may be expected to work in the middle of the night. TV is a twenty-four-hour-a-day business, and as a recent hire, chances are you'll start on a weird shift. My schedule is a perfect example. The people on my crew put together the early morning news, local cut-ins into network news, and the noon show. That means some of us have to get to work at three-thirty in the morning, Monday through Friday. It sounds like hell, I know, and after a late night out, it is. But if you do get this shift, you also get off work at lunchtime, have your afternoons and evenings to yourself, and are rarely asked to come in on a weekend. You also work under minimal supervision. Managers don't stroll in until nine-thirty or so, and even when they are around, they tend to be a little more easygoing. After all, they probably feel a little guilty because they know you were slaving away at work while everyone else was sound asleep.

Don't worry about dozing off, though; there's nothing more stressful than live television. Every day you're under extreme deadline pressure, because whether you've finished your work or not, the show goes on at the same time. However, this isn't necessarily a negative. Let's be honest, lots of us do our best work under the gun. In college, in fact, some of my best papers were written at the very last minute. So if any of you can relate to this kind of pressure, it might be a positive for you, too.

THE GOOD DAYS

If you like excitement, there's nothing like being in a newsroom when news breaks. The earthquake in Southern California . . . the burning of the Russian parliament building . . . the mass suicide at Waco, Texas. To know you control what people hear is incredibly empowering. Whether you're researching facts, typing up those crawl messages that run at the bottom of the screen, or rolling the TelePrompTer, you're a part of it all. And when a really big story hits, it makes you realize how many people depend on you and how important your work really is. Here's an example:

When I first moved to California, the state hadn't seen serious rain in years, but my first year on the job, the Golden State received more rain in a month than it had in the previous seven years put together. And right in the middle of one of the fiercest storms, my partner happened to call in sick, making me the only PA at the station. Heavy rains were flooding rivers, making roads slick, and causing mud slides. The Emergency Broadcasting System had ordered us to flash a warning on the air immediately, and it was up to me to make it happen.

Had I ever done one before? Yes. The thing was, would I remember how? I had never had to do one all by myself. No one else at the station could do it, we didn't have time to call in another PA, and it had to go on the air immediately. I took a deep breath and quickly typed up the message. Then I pressed what I hoped were the right buttons and waited for the results. An Emergency Broad-casting System message began to creep along the bottom of the screen. It worked! And no typos, either! After a quick thumbs-up from my executive producer, I called master control. When he said "Go," I called up the crawl again, and this time it appeared on every television set in the newsroom that was tuned in to our station. I was beaming. Everyone who was watching our channel at that moment in the entire Bay Area would learn which roads were flooded and what precautions they needed to take. Millions of people were watching my handiwork. I might even have saved some lives—not to mention my job. I ended up staying there five more hours, typing up crawl messages and flashing the words across the screen. I glanced up at a TV tuned to another station and saw the same crawl message. Somewhere out there, another PA was doing the same thing I was. I just hope her grin was as wide as mine.

THE BAD DAYS

There are also days when smiling is the last thing I feel like doing. News is inherently unpredictable, which means that as much as you try to make the right decisions, it's impossible to be right all of the time. Sometimes the little feature story you think is irrelevant balloons into the biggest story of the day. Other times the story you expect to lead the show fizzles into nothing. It's a guessing game and sometimes you make the wrong call. And if that isn't enough, imagine making the wrong call in front of millions of people. It happened to me.

It seemed like it was going to go the way of most mornings. I came in a little after three-thirty, grabbed a cup of burned coffee from the kitchenette, mumbled an apology to my producer, jumped up to the assignment desk, threw my bag on the ground, and sat down. I cranked up the volume on the scanners, logged on to the computer, and scanned the wires for big news. Nothing. There rarely is overnight: a couple of shootings, a carjacking, or maybe a small fire. That's pretty much it. Good. I could handle this.

Suddenly I heard over the scanner, "We got a big one here. We're going to need some help." It was coming from the Belmont Fire Department, about half an hour south of San Francisco. I went back to the wires. "Belmont firefighters reported to the scene of a three-alarm fire at a paint warehouse at 3:40 A.M. The second story of the three-story building is engulfed in flames." Paint factories are highly explosive, and so, potentially, was the story. Uh-oh. I called the Belmont Fire Department to confirm. Yes, there was a fire. Yes, it was raging out of control. Yes, it was a paint factory. No injuries had been reported. I gave the information to my producer, then checked the wires again. The fire rating had been increased to four alarms. I called the fire department again, but the dispatcher was too busy to talk to me and hung up. It was a biggie. The fire jumped to five alarms. My producer told me to start waking people up, beginning with the managing editor. "No apology necessary," he said. "Just get chopper five and a crew up there, and send another reporter to the site."

So this was for real. The producer dumped a couple of stories and reformatted the show with a two-minute live shot devoted to the fire. I called the fire department to check on the status of the blaze, but to my dismay, I found out they were getting a handle on the fire. I had a sinking feeling in the pit of my stomach. What if the firefighters put out the fire before we went on the air? We'd have a two-minute nonstory at the top of the show. But it was too late to back out now. Naturally I hoped the firefighters would put out the fire before anyone got hurt, but couldn't they wait until six-thirty?

When I called the fire department again, I was told that it was 80 percent contained. Just then the pilot called and said he was at the airport and ready to go. Realizing it would end up being a waste of money, I canceled the chopper order and told the extra crew to go back to sleep. But it was only half an hour to show time. There was no time to rewrite the show or to send our crew to another site. At six o'clock we went on the air, with the extinguished fire as our lead story. I can still hear the anchor now: "A large paint warehouse in Belmont broke into flames early this morning. Our reporter is live at the site. What's the latest?" "Well, as you can see, the fire is out now, but . . ." What a morning. While all of the other stations were covering whatever real news was happening, our reporter was standing in the dark in front of an old warehouse, and I was the one who had sent him there.

THE NEWS SUMMARY

While you have to take the bad with the good, there's still plenty of good to chirp about. Unlike other businesses, where you compete with your peers, broadcast news is the product of people working together. It has to be, because each person is judged not by his or her individual efforts but by the quality of the show as a whole. When you're going to work every day, believe me, it's great to work *with* your coworkers and not against them.

So what does all of this mean to you? Well, if you like identifying issues and explaining them to people, if you like telling stories and think you tell them well, and if the pressure doesn't bother you or even secretly titillates you in some weird way, broadcast news may be the field for you.

There is a serious element to this job—freedom of the press is an important matter. The public has a right to keep its governing body in check, and being a part of that is a real responsibility. At the same time, though, it's an enjoyable responsibility. If there's one thing that distinguishes my day from those of my friends, I'd have to say it's that I actually look forward to going to work. Part of the reason is the people, part of it's the job. But mostly it is the atmosphere—it's fun, it's crazy, and it's totally unpredictable. Just like life.

Some Advice from Samantha

News Experience: TV stations are considered the glamorous, but trashy, cousin to print, so if you want to come across as a serious newshound, getting some articles published in your college newspaper can definitely help. If you can get broadcasting experience in college, so much the better.

Broadcast Experience: Most college radio stations are known for their music, but they're also a great place to start in news. Some schools also have student-run television stations. If you can get your foot in there, you'll be in great shape.

The Interview: Realize where you're interviewing, and dress appropriately. TV news is not a traditional field, so leave your navy pinstripe at home. Wear a suit if you have one, but try to pick something really fashionable, especially if you're a woman. The newsroom is a casual and fun environment, so dress in a way that reflects those qualities.

Trade Associations: Trade associations can be very helpful. The Radio and Television News Directors Association (RTNDA) hosts weekend symposiums for people working in the field. The conferences usually include a forum on getting started, with a panel of local news directors available for questions.

Internships: If at all possible, try to get an internship before you graduate. I can't stress this enough. It's simply the best way to get hands-on experience at a real station, test whether or not you really want to enter the business, and, most important, make contacts. Unlike more traditional businesses, broadcast news facilities don't have a seasonal recruiting process. In fact, they don't recruit at all. If the station has an opening for an entry-level position, the first place they look is their pool of interns. If they don't have an opening, at least you'll then know people in the business who can help you with your job search or write letters on your behalf. The easiest places to look for internships are in your hometown and your college town, or the closest city to either place.

A Few Resources to Help You Out

Working in TV News: The Insider's Guide, by Carl Filoreto and Lynn Setzer (Memphis: Mustang Publishing, 1993). A look at the daily life of TV journalists, information on internships, job descriptions, salaries, advice on résumés and tapes, and a complete listing of addresses of every TV station with a news department in the United States and Canada.

Making It in Broadcasting: An Insider's Guide to Career Opportunities, by Leonard Mogel (New York: Collier Books/Macmillan, 1993). This resource provides detailed explanations of how the business works and the roles people play. It also includes interviews with industry insiders, job-finding tips, and internship listings.

Women's Bureau, U.S. Department of Labor (200 Constitution Avenue NW, Washington, D.C. 20210). Write to this address for a free copy of *Women on the Job*, a book put together by the Department of Labor and the American Women in Radio and Television to assist women considering careers in electronic media.

Radio and Television News Directors Association (1717 K Street NW, Suite 615, Washington, D.C. 20006, [202] 659-6510). RTNDA publishes a biweekly job bulletin, sponsors regional conferences, and offers other career development assistance. Call or write about student membership information.

Broadcasting and Cable (P.O. Box 6399, Torrance, Calif. 90504). At $117 a year, this magazine is probably not something you will subscribe to, but it may be worth looking for at the library or a well-stocked bookstore. At the back of each issue is a classified section that includes job listings.

Landing a

Magazine

Internship

Shanti Menon

Writing for a magazine is one avenue for recent graduates who want to write and get paid to do it. In this essay, Shanti describes her serendipitous entry into the industry and then sheds some light on the day-to-day role she played as an intern for *Discover* magazine.

The highlight of my job search was telling the managing editor of *People* magazine how my résumé ended up on her desk. "Your brother's car salesman is my father's patient," I told her.

A shady but lovable character, my father's patient was a former limo driver (and small-time mafioso, we think) who would often disappear for weeks at a time and resurface later under a different name. He was always stopping by the house with week-old flowers for my mother or Bears T-shirts for my brother and me. Sometimes he would offer my father a good deal on a Rolex. So when he said, "Shanti's looking for a job in magazines? I'll take care of it," I never really expected anything to come of it—just as the managing editor of *People* never expected anything to come of chatting with her brother's car salesman at a Christmas party.

With that sort of introduction, *People* couldn't forget me. A month later they offered me an opportunity to work as a freelancer on the "50 Best and Worst Dressed" issue. To the disappointment of many of my friends, I turned them down, because by that time I had received an offer for a paid internship at *Discover*, a popular science magazine.

How did I go from hot fashion to cold fusion, you ask? Two discoveries propelled me. First, I found out that magazine editors are less concerned with your knowledge of subject matter than in your ability to string a sentence together, be it about astrophysics or hair care of the stars. Just as important, I learned that finding a real job at a magazine with little or no experience wasn't going to be easy, so any paid internship was worth considering.

I looked for jobs with all kinds of magazines. I interviewed with personnel departments at the more "glamorous" magazines, where even in my interview suit I felt like the receptionist looked more professional than I did. At a weekly newsmagazine, the research director helpfully suggested that I move to Washington, D.C., and work for an Indian newspaper before coming back to him. "Call me," he said. "I'd be really interested to know how you're doing." In other words, with no entry-level positions open, they weren't interested in me. When I actually received an offer from *Discover*, it seemed too good to pass up.

As I learned during my search, the publishing industry is big on "paying dues." Any sort of entry-level position usually has a heavy dose of clerical work, and you have to put in at least a year or two before you can dump that work on someone else. The other positions I was looking at were either unpaid internships that entailed a good amount of responsibility but offered no guarantee of a permanent position, or ones that involved developing a close personal relationship with the copy machine and wearing a sign that said "Kick me, I'm the intern." Although I would have taken one of those positions just to get my foot in the door, I was lucky enough to find an internship that was paid (a laughable amount for New York City, but paid, just the same) and where I actually got to write. Except for the number of zeros on my paycheck and the fact that I was occasionally asked to "do something" about our increasingly disheveled library, I was treated pretty much like any other member of the staff.

Although popular science didn't immediately come to mind when I thought about writing for a magazine, I had nothing against science. As a Russian studies major, I voluntarily took several science classes in college, but only with the intent of bettering my mind. I certainly wasn't expecting to make a career out of it.

After four years of college, I was not certain what I planned to make my career. I came away from a fascinating summer in Russia knowing I never wanted to live there, even though I enjoyed learning about it. I toyed with the idea of grad school, but I couldn't imagine having to study only a single subject. I realized that what I liked was the whole learning process. I liked reading, digesting, analyzing, and processing information. I knew I could write, but I was sure that the frenetic pace and high pressure of writing for a daily newspaper wasn't suited for my temperament. As for sitting down and writing the Great American Novel, well, I wasn't quite ready for that either. So after six months of working as a temp and traveling, I moved to New York to look for a job in publishing. Luckily, I had several relatives in the area who were used to people showing up on their doorstep and announcing they had come to stay, so I didn't have to worry about where I was going to sleep while I was out job hunting.

JUST THE FACTS, MA'AM

A lot of newcomers to magazine publishing start out purely as fact checkers. Although I was given a mix of responsibilities, this was a big part of my job, too. It's sort of magazine quality control, making sure all of the factual information in an article is correct. Sometimes the writer may have misunderstood something, or sometimes the editor, in his or her constant struggle to shorten the length of a piece, may inadvertently change its meaning.

As an intern, before fact checking any article, you will usually read up on all of the information the writer used in writing it, so you're familiar with the material. If something is wrong, you've got to understand why it's wrong and how to change it, so you can explain it to the editor. Fact checking also requires a certain amount of tact. You're trying to get sources to confirm factual information without letting them edit the article so they come off sounding good, which they invariably attempt to do. You also have to be able to paraphrase what's being said without changing the meaning of the passage. If, for example, I'm fact checking an article on something like physics, which was never my strong point, I just cross my fingers and pray the scientist will be patient with me. Usually they are. Once I had a long chat with a Polish theoretical physicist who was extremely kind and pleasant and really took time to explain things to me. He couldn't have been nicer. Later I discovered that I had received a brief course in gravitational microlensing from a man who was up for a Nobel Prize.

Sometimes the editor may want to add a bit of information to the article to spice it up. It becomes the fact checker's job to obtain such material. For a piece on tiny bits of junk in space that can damage satellites, my editor wanted to find out how thick the walls of the space shuttle were. The researcher who had been interviewed for the article didn't know, so I called NASA. They didn't know. They referred me to Rockwell International, which builds the shuttles. No one there could tell me either. A few of the editors here are chummy with astronaut Buzz Aldrin. Buzz didn't know. I was forced to report to my editor that *nobody knows* how thick the walls of the space shuttle are.

Very rarely are fact checkers allowed to get away with claiming there's just no way to find something out—someone eventually told me how thick the windows in the shuttle were, so we used that fact instead. When you do get hold of an elusive fact, like how many licks it takes to get to the center of a Tootsie Roll Pop, or in my case, how many generations it takes to breed a better banana, fact checking can be rewarding, even if your efforts are underappreciated. There are times I'm convinced that I have saved a piece from embarrassing the magazine and misleading millions of readers—Irian Jaya is part of Indonesia, not Malaysia—but the only people who usually know what I've done are the editor, the writer, and the scientist.

JUST THE FAX, THE MAIL, AND A COUPLE OF ARTICLES, MA'AM

Aside from fact checking, my other duties as an intern were opening the mail for the senior news editor and writing a couple of stories each month. All of our shorter articles are written in-house and the editors usually assign stories from what we propose each month. This is where opening the mail came in handy. About half of it is junk, but the rest is press releases from universities and big laboratories, telling us what projects their scientists are working on and what new discoveries they've made. Some of them are sheer propaganda, but others contain newsworthy items that could make a great story. Another way to find out what's new in the world of science is to flip through journals such as *Science* and *Nature*, which publish original papers by scientists. These are often laced with academic jargon and barely readable to the lay person. How can you hope to make it through an article when its title alone is something as unwieldy as "Crystal Structure of the Catalytic Domain of HIV-1 Integrase: Similarity to Other Polynucleotidal Transferases"? Most people, myself included, are intimidated or turned off by such technical speak. But after a few weeks on the job, I realized that I could turn that paper into a brief, punchy article called "New Approach for AIDS Drug." Now, that's something people may want to read about.

PUTTING IT ALL TOGETHER

The deadline pressure isn't as intense at a monthly magazine as it is at a daily newspaper. I had trouble adjusting at first to the idea that we were writing the April issue in mid-January, but when I

realized what was involved in putting an article together, it all made sense. We normally have almost two weeks to write our stories, usually about three each issue. As in writing on any subject, this involves reading up on background material, formulating some questions, and then interviewing the appropriate party. Since, contrary to popular opinion here, news doesn't occur only in New York City, I conduct these interviews over the phone.

After the stories are submitted, there's a lull while the senior editors do their "editing." I put "editing" in quotes because the edited version of my first article was actually a complete rewrite done by my editor. This was discouraging at first, because the editors rarely have time to sit down and tell you how to improve your writing and reporting skills. I had to learn by doing, and the more articles I wrote, the more I found I was absorbing the style of the magazine.

When I left college, I thought I knew how to write clearly and concisely, but I was at *Discover* about five months before I could claim that an article was truly mine.

After editing, the stories that I didn't write go to me for fact checking, back to the editor for corrections, to the editor in chief for a top edit, and to the copy editor for the final version. After that, the news section gets laid out and we see about three more versions of it before the magazine gets shipped out to the printer. The April issue hits the newsstands in the third week of March.

Because of the cyclical nature of the job, there's some downtime. Every month there are about three days of boredom while the editors deal with a backlog of work, but as soon as that's done, it all gets dumped on me. Then there are about three weeks of frenzied activity before it tapers off again.

Moving Up

After six months as an intern, as the security deposit on my first apartment was coming due and I started hunting for a real job with a real salary, a permanent position at *Discover* opened up for a researcher/reporter. In this new position, I'm getting a chance to write longer articles with bylines, but I also still have to do fact checking.

Though sitting at a desk in front of a computer all day can be tedious, my job is hardly dull. I just love the fact that I'm out of school but still learning. It's one of the best things about working in magazines—whether you're involved in popular science, home gardening, women's fashion, or foreign policy, you can indulge yourself in that subject. The world I've been immersed in here has ranged from the mystical, like the quest of some theoretical physicists to explain the universe; to the practical, such as the development of a quieter vacuum cleaner; to the bizarre, as was my discussion with two researchers about the copulation calls of female baboons. I really do learn something new every day. And I've become a formidable, if perhaps slightly eclectic, conversationalist—people never know when I'm going to start talking about bugs and mummies. I'm still not convinced I want to stick to science writing, but when the time comes to move on, I'll have built up enough clips to demonstrate my experience and writing abilities. Maybe someday I'll find the magazine that's the perfect combination of *Discover*, *Spin*, the *Economist*, and *Ms*. And hopefully I'll find someone who knows someone whose father's car salesman is the husband of the editor in chief.

Some Advice from Shanti

Where to Start: Start sending résumés to the magazines you read, like, and know about. If, like most college students, you don't have time to read magazines regularly, go to a library or bookstore and check out the periodicals section. You won't believe how many magazines are out there.

Whom to Contact: If you're looking at a big company, try to send your résumé directly to a senior editor or an editor in charge of a particular section of the magazine where you're interested in working. It will probably be forwarded to the human resource department, but perhaps before it gets there, some editor will have scribbled a comment on it in your favor.

Don't Forget the Little Guys: Think globally, act locally. There are plenty of other magazines besides the national ones. Although your ultimate goal may be to become a regular columnist for *Rolling Stone*, you may have a better chance getting a start at a smaller, local magazine, or even a newsletter. In a smaller office with fewer staff members, you'll usually get the opportunity to learn more about how all of the departments interact. You'll also be rewarded with greater responsibilities than you might working within a large corporation, where employees tend to be more territorial and competitive.

Know the Magazine: Before your interview, or even if you're just writing a cover letter, know who you're dealing with. What have they written about lately? (A little flattery never hurts.) Read up on the last several issues so that you're familiar with the style and structure of the magazine.

Which department is your favorite? What article did you like, or not like, recently, and why? Do you think the magazine can be improved? How?

Make It Easier on Yourself: If you have an opportunity to get some sort of experience in magazines, journalism, or publishing before you start looking for a job, do it! Also, the more clips you have, the better. Try submitting freelance articles to a small publication near your home or school.

New York City: Regardless of your feelings toward The City (being from Chicago, I had to hate it), New York is where many of the major publishing companies and magazines are located. Time-Warner, Condé Nast—they're all there. This doesn't mean that you can't look anywhere else, but for the sheer volume of opportunity, New York is a good place to be.

Courses: You may see various prestigious colleges like Radcliffe offering summer programs in publishing and magazine journalism. These courses are very good at introducing you to potential contacts as well as offering you an "in" into the industry. If you can afford to spend several thousand dollars on a six-to-eight-week course, it can make the job search a little easier.

Round Up the Troops! Get everyone you know to help find you a job— relatives, friends, friends of friends, recent alumni. The more people you talk to about your interests and career goals, the greater the possibility you'll find someone who's tapped into the publishing world and can tell you about an opening. The people who already have jobs generally hear about openings before they're listed in the want ads.

A Few Resources to Help You Out

American Society of Magazine Editors (575 Lexington Avenue, New York, N.Y. 10022, [212] 752-0055). Although ASME doesn't offer student memberships, it does publish *Careers in Magazine Publishing*, a booklet to help college students and recent graduates interested in magazine publishing, and has an internship placement program.

Magazines Career Directory, edited by Bradley J. Morgan (Detroit: Visible Ink, 1993). Includes industry insiders' perspectives on various career paths, advice on conducting a job search in magazine publishing, and a listing of close to two hundred magazines and publishers that offer entry-level magazine jobs and internships.

Writer's Market (Cincinnati: Writers Digest Books, 1994). A comprehensive reference guide for writers looking to get published. It contains information on more than four thousand publishers (consumer magazines, trade journals, book publishers) to whom you may consider selling your articles, books, short stories, and so forth.

Get Published: 100 Top Magazine Editors Tell You How, by Diane Gage and Marcia Coppess (New York: Owl Books/Henry Holt, 1994). This well-researched book gives you the inside scoop on everything from *Reader's Digest* to *Black Enterprise*. You can find out what kind of articles each magazine is looking for, how much they pay, and how to slant your ideas to cater to each publication. Highly recommended.

Playing in

a Band

Ben Davis

Ever wonder what would happen if you tried to keep that college band together after graduation or formed a new one once you're out in the "real world"? Well, here are the reflections of one musician who's following that dream.

I have this old R.E.M. record. It's from a show they played in 1981—before any studio recordings—and it does not sound like the work of an ambitious group of songwriters, international pop stars, or corporate heads of film production companies. It's a band you'd enjoy at a frat party but feel a little sorry for at a bar.

I am twenty-four and have played in various bands since junior high. Most of the music I've made induces a similar combination of embarrassment and awe. I am now in a band I consider serious and sometimes even think is very good. I am also a college graduate unsure of how or when I will enter what many would call my "professional" life. If you would have asked me ten years ago, I probably would have had just enough foresight to answer, "No, I'll probably be too busy to play music by the time I get to college." Along with most of the world, I recognize that conven-

tional careers last longer than rock 'n' roll bands. I know I won't
do this forever, but I also know there's nothing else I'd rather do
right now.

Although there are many musicians who can afford *not* to work
outside of their trade, I am not (yet) one of them. A career in a
symphony, playing on TV commercial or film soundtracks, doing
session work in studios, teaching lessons—none of these routes
strongly appeals to me, and I wouldn't pretend to be master enough
of any instrument to pursue them. I'm a sucker for purity. I'm in
this to write, play, and record original songs. Anyway, there's no
cheaper therapy around. What this means in the world of rent and
groceries is that without a record deal or some kind of financial
backing, I'm at risk of having my musical career called a hobby.

During my first year of college, I borrowed a friend's Tascam
Porta-One (four-track recorder). It was the first time I'd tried to

write songs. I went to a soundproof practice room at the music school and mostly recorded as I wrote, mumbling into a cheap microphone that I set down across my notebook on a music stand. It wasn't too far removed from the strategically placed boom box in our high school garages. I sent the tape to a handful of friends. It took three years of recording and playing my songs for other people before I found compatible players who wanted to form a band.

As a trio—an upright and electric bass player, a fiddler and mandolinist, and myself on guitar—we worked at becoming comfortable with one another's songs, started writing together, and went through two drummers before we finally met someone who really fit. Playing around school and at a few clubs, we got attention from the local press, won a Battle of the Bands, and got the kind of people who go and jump around at shows to come and jump around at our shows.

For our first tape, we rented an eight-track for a week, recruited a friend to help us engineer, and recorded seventeen songs. After laying basic tracks (bass, drums, and guitar, in this case), we moved the studio into my apartment, and for the next five days of overdubs and practice mixes, we attended only a few classes, didn't see any friends, and slept very little. For the final mix, we went back to our practice space, and for twenty hours straight, we finished what became our first tape. A few months later, we were selling tapes at shows and we had reviews in the local papers (photocopies of which we still put in our promo packages).

The freedom of being involved in a band (without a proper manager, booking agent, attorney, or record label) goes far beyond the opportunities of escaping a conventional forty-hour workweek. Like owning a small business, the work we do is entirely for ourselves. We put together the recordings, send the packages to clubs in different cities, and call them incessantly to arrange shows. Months later we drive into a city (often for the first time) with a nearly empty schedule, performing for new sets of ears in clubs, on the street, and on an occasional radio show.

Left his day job behind ... every fool dies trying, to get his back ... —The Jayhawks, "Nevada, California"

I think most young musicians, writers, and other artists must prepare themselves for some level of instability—financially or otherwise. In some eyes, your part-time job at the café or even as a bank teller means a lack of ambition. To others, your ability to work on your art and support yourself at the same time shows courage and tenacity. It takes a long time to build a dazzling portfolio and gain enough recognition to ensure that your art will sustain your financially. Many great artists never quit their day jobs. Rent must be paid, and one has to sacrifice time and energy that could be spent more creatively. But for many people leaving the security of college, a little instability can be a welcome change, and they'll muster up the resilience to cope. And for students who held jobs during school, they're already familiar with the juggling act.

For me, one of the biggest sacrifices has been putting aside potential full-time jobs in other fields of interest. To allow for touring, I've needed a job that pays well and gives me time off whenever needed. I'm paying rent while away, of course, and I've watched all of the money I saved from college jobs quickly disappear during these times. But it *has* worked so far. I'm a freelance techie for an audio-visual company, and I'm lucky enough to be paid more than I would for slinging coffee or selling socks. Also, I've spent a quarter of the past year out of town and I do still *have* my job. But setting up video monitors and slide projectors is not the most rewarding part of my life.

On a small scale, gigging, and even recording independently, can be profitable. We've broken even on tours (all two of them) when we consider promotional costs, gas money, phone bills for booking, making cassettes to sell at shows, and everything else.

More important than the infrequent financial rewards, at the early stages in particular, are the many experiences gained. Some would like to call this "life education." In the music business, this is especially true. If you take an active role in the promotion of your music (or are forced to for lack of outside support), you inevitably gain valuable experience in the industry. Talking with record label people and other musicians and managers, I've learned about music marketing strategies and the A & R (artist and repertoire) culture that hunts and gathers new talent. After spending every other day on the phone for months at a time, I've acquired more experience than I ever would have wanted booking tours. I have collected a pile of research in entertainment law and am still working through it to prepare for all of the slimy schemes and sticky situations to come. And since we've done nearly all of our recordings by ourselves, I've gained more practical experience in recording engineering than I could have in a year of making coffee and answering phones as an intern at a major studio.

Beyond these immediate gratifications, though, are much more lasting benefits derived from the whole process of writing, performing, and recording. Many of the professionals who work in the industry are former rockers. I think it only makes them more sensitive to their own place in the game when they have personal experience with the other players. I was a deejay in college, another related experience that has made me better informed: I know how easily promotional CDs can end up in the dollar bin of local record stores after a quick listen from impatient reviewers. If you have any interest in the business of music other than being a face on MTV, then promoting and working your band is an excellent way to learn.

> *I have no need to let the neighbors run my life, no-oh, no-oh . . .*
> —Jonathan Richman, "Neighbors"

So what *is* everybody else doing? Of course it's on your mind. That woman down the hall with the computer science degree who's designing software for Apple, the scrawny kid from Minnesota working at the White House . . . does it matter? If you're comfortable with whatever yardsticks you use to measure your own projects or prospects, it shouldn't.

A friend of a friend of a friend auditioned for the saxophone spot on the Rolling Stones' *Voodoo Lounge* tour, and got it. His parents can't stop sharing this with the rest of the world. They threw a party in their son's honor. He's thirty. I have a suspicion that until that phone call ("Mom, guess what!") his parents were wondering when the kid would grow up and get on with his life. Rock 'n' roll isn't number one on the list of what parents rush to tell their friends about.

Having completed a semiprofessional recording that we're all very proud of, we're now entering the tense and taxing period of courting record labels and a small group of other important ears in the industry. It's a step we've each been working toward even before we met and started playing together. When we hear from the labels, we might decide to start looking for more modest goals. Or we could be on our way to being heard by far more people than we are now.

Two of the members in the band are now in their final year of school. The other three of us are living, breathing, working world people, and the tension between our very different responsibilities has made our sticking together remarkable. The three of us who must work to pay the rent, however, are much more concerned with becoming a financially viable band if we are going to continue making investments of time, energy, and money. But regardless of what responses we get, I'm confident that we'll all continue writing and playing in some form or another. Sending four-track projects to friends once or twice a year would still be an ambitious and rewarding undertaking.

You're only as good as your knees . . .
—Joe Henry, "Short Man's Room"

The music business is a lot like professional sports—something of an adolescent dream where financial success is limited to a very few who make very much. You have to be extremely good and extremely marketable (you don't get paid unless you're both), and if by some stroke of misfortune you don't "make it," you'd better have something to fall back on (or rise up to). Colleges use a minimum GPA as eligibility for sports. One reason is that you'll have a degree and thus some means of supporting yourself when "the knees go." No such regulation exists in the music industry, and there are former stars still paying advances back to their record companies for unsuccessful albums. Some of these musicians now consider themselves lucky to be in a successful wedding band. They probably should.

With the exception of the Rolling Stones and a few others, pop musicians come and go very quickly. Most bands riding any current wave of popularity now will, in ten years, have exhausted themselves mentally or physically, be so unfairly treated by their record company that they flee the industry, or be so blessed as to discover something more meaningful. But don't try telling any of them that now. (Certainly don't try telling *me*.) On the other hand, poll would-have-been musicians at age forty and you might find some regrets about not pursuing their music. And there are very few junior executives who retire at forty to begin a musical career. If I were writing as that regretful forty-year-old, I have a strong suspicion that I would be encouraging young musicians and songwriters to rock on.

In the summer of last year, we spent two weeks at a farm in Kankakee, Illinois. The bass player's grandmother owns the place: a small cottage and an enormous old barn converted to serve as a meeting room for local businesses, a venue for community events, and various performances. A huge deck connected to the main room looked out over soy fields straight ahead, rows of trees along the banks of the Kankakee River on one side, and a two-lane road that disappeared at the top of a hill on the other. We came with two carloads of instruments, a rented PA, and two weeks' worth of groceries. I was bringing a friend to play with the band for the first time, and we hid ourselves away to work on new songs and arrangements before beginning our next recording project. The scenery and the solitude were inspiring, and the work we did those two weeks led to the recordings we now use for our demo package. There certainly wasn't anyone commending our practicality or wisdom in taking two weeks' vacation time, paid or unpaid, to go to an empty barn in the middle of summer. I happen to think it was a wise move, maybe even a necessary one.

If you're having fun, rock on. If it lasts, great; if it grows, great; if not, you've done it, get on with your life. I don't think of music as a vocation. Some people do. But when we spend ten hours on a mix that finally comes together, when I'm writing well and the group works up new songs that sound right, it's a satisfaction I find nowhere else. When I don't and we don't, I hope I'll be able to stop and move on.

Some Advice from Ben

Recording: Equipment rentals are cheap. Compared to going into a studio to record, renting an eight-track cassette or digital tape recorder is a far more economical way to get a decent recording to sell at shows or give to friends. Buy a book on home recording if you've never done it before or find someone who has (a friend who'll do it for a six-pack will do fine) to help you. Doing a home recording will also help keep you from wasting time (and, therefore, lots of money) when you do eventually record in a studio.

Mailing Lists: Building a fan base is important. A mailing list does not accomplish that, but it does give you a means of reaching them. Send out postcards when you have shows coming up. Everybody wins—your friends and fans will know about your gigs and the clubs you play will draw a bigger crowd, which helps you get invited back. And unless you happen to have distribution through Tower Records, mailing lists are also essential for letting people know when you have a new tape or CD.

Booking Shows: When you're trying to establish yourself, it's important to target clubs whose clientele are likely to be receptive to your music. Take a look at what other bands have played at the venue. If they've booked band X and Y, who have a similar sound, maybe they'll also want you. Other bands can be helpful in suggesting places.

Being Involved in the Business Side: I've heard it said that musicians who serve as their own manager are taken seriously as neither. The business side of things exercised a part of my brain I needed to exercise, so it has worked for me. But if it's not your thing, don't do it. There's nothing wrong with staying focused exclusively on your music. Find a friend who will do the calling for tours or send packages to labels. It will simplify your life and it will help your credibility.

Networking: You don't have to call it that, but you do have to do it. There's no point in learning everything by trial and error if you can benefit from what others have already learned. Talking to other bands is one of the most effective ways to find out which venues will treat you well and will have good attendance, receptive crowds, and so on. Also, find out what bands are on what labels and ask them how they're treated and what channels got them in touch with the label.

A Few Resources to Help You Out

The Business of Music: A Practical Guide to the Music Industry for Publishers, Writers, Record Companies, Producers, Artists, Agents, by Sidney Shemel and M. William Krasilovsky (New York: Billboard Publications, 1990). Known to many as the industry bible, this thorough guide addresses recording artist contracts, music videos, agents and managers, trade associations, copyright law, and more.

All You Need to Know About the Music Business, by Donald S. Passman (New York: Simon and Schuster, 1994). Savvy insider's guide to every legal and financial facet of the business. "Should be required reading for anyone planning or enduring a career in the Biz" (*Rolling Stone*).

The Billboard Guide to Home Recording, by Ray Baragary (New York: Billboard Books/Watson-Guptill Publications, 1990). A handbook of recording techniques and equipment options, explaining the basics of making high-quality tapes and demos in a home studio setup.

Writing Scripts

---

and Telling Lies

Dave Story

Trying to write screenplays for a living is kind of like waking up every morning and buying a lottery ticket. Each day the odds are against you, yet you keep trying anyway. Dave is one writer who could not ignore his desire to tell stories. On these pages, he shares a little of his own.

I love telling lies. It's why I'm a writer—specifically, a screenwriter. As any kid can tell you, lying is all about making up stories that stretch the imagination but don't defy belief. The same goes for writing for film.

I grew up with a watchful and vengeful twin brother, so I was never able to lie to my parents like most kids. Instead I sought out more socially acceptable ways to lie. I wrote short stories about monkeys and treehouses, staged plays about the Easter Bunny in my basement, and eventually made super 8 movies. While the rest of my junior high classmates were writing dully factual papers about World War II, I lobbied my teacher to let me make a super 8 spoof of *The Guns of Navarone*. The movie was full of the most puerile humor and atrocious wordplay imaginable, but my classmates loved it. Their reaction made me want to be a liar for life.

Still, when I went to college, I figured it was time to put away
the lies, get serious, and think about finding a job. But I couldn't
shake the bug. After speaking with a film professor, I decided to
study cinema. I can still see the surprise on my football coach's
face when I told him I would need to miss two practices every
week so I could watch movies. Of course, being obsessed with
movies in college doesn't necessarily lead to work in the outside
world. When I graduated, I really had to decide whether I could
make movies my career. That is where lying comes in handy. You
have to lie to yourself by saying that the nearly insurmountable
odds against achieving your dream don't mean a damn thing. It's
an important step, one that anyone who's chasing his or her dream
must take. If you start to believe you don't have a chance, you
probably won't.

My next step toward becoming a filmmaker was to move to New
York and find work as a production assistant. It's not hard for
bright, energetic college grads to become PAs in the New York
film world. But I quickly found that it is tough to move off the
production track once you're on it. After observing location scouts,
assistant directors, unit production managers, and line producers,
I realized that no matter how well they were doing their jobs, they
were only helping to realize someone else's vision. Working on a
movie set was invaluable training for me, and I'd recommend it as
a start for anyone considering joining the movie business, but after
a while I realized I'd have to keep moving if I was going to be able
to tell my lies.

HEADING WEST

From what I could glean from reading interviews with people who'd
made it in film—producers, directors, and executives—it seemed
that the best way to break into the movie business was by writing.
So when a college buddy in film school in Los Angeles offered his
lumpy couch for a few weeks, I packed up and moved to Hollywood. Now, there's no shortage of liars and wanna-be liars in

Hollywood. I was smart enough to realize that my college attempts at filmmaking and writing weren't going to knock any studio executives out of their seats. I figured I should first learn everything I could about the craft of screenwriting.

In the meantime, I needed to eat. Through the want ads I found a job recruiting movie viewers to partake in market research screenings. It was hard, exhausting, and often frustrating work, but it paid well and I could do it at night and on weekends while I learned about screenwriting during the day. I scanned how-to books, attended lectures, and watched movies until I felt comfortable analyzing how a script is written. During this time, I started but then abandoned several screenplays because my ideas never seemed to fit my newly found standards of what makes a good movie. In other words, I felt like I was being a bit of a fake—I was in Hollywood to write scripts, but all I had been doing was learning about them. I wondered whether I should have just pursued a job in advertising instead.

Through good fortune and hard work, I eventually landed a job writing script "coverage" for the International Creative Management (ICM) talent agency. In the movie industry, to "cover" a script is to briefly synopsize its plot and then analyze whether it would make a good movie. Coverage is used by busy studio executives and agents when they need to be informed of scripts they might not have the time to read. Although at first I was worried that reading ten scripts a week would diminish my own writing, I found out that the job was more educational than I ever dreamed it would be. Sure, it was exhausting to be always reading and writing about movies, but it taught me innumerable lessons. Being exposed to so many scripts made it easy to distinguish between effective and ineffective writing. I made note of which techniques, rhythms, and story approaches captured my attention and which caused my interest to wane—critical knowledge for someone hoping to someday have his work before the eyes of those busy studio executives. I put these lessons to use during the writing of my first full-length script, a modern-day comic western.

ROOKIE WRITER

Except for *City Slickers*, modern-day comic westerns aren't known for being boffo box office draws. Still, I felt good about my story. I came up with some taut sequences, some memorable characters, and some witty dialogue. Finishing that first script was an exhilarating feeling. I knew I had put my best effort into something creative and I hoped the response to my work would meet my expectations. Of course, after working as a script reader, I had no illusions about the difficulty of selling a script. I was reading scores of screenplays a month and only a minuscule number were actually being made into movies. Most of the scripts I read that ended up being produced were solid. Yet I was stunned that turkeys also ended up making it to the big screen. I realized that Hollywood's not a meritocracy. Getting produced is a game of luck, a game of chance. I was ready to send my script out onto the playing field to participate in the game.

Now, I've already told you my reasons for getting into this line of work. Unlike a lot of the clods who come out to Hollywood, I wasn't in it just for the money. Sure, screenwriting money is enticing, but if that's your only reason for writing, then believe me, you'd do better in Vegas. No, what I wanted was to recapture the thrill I got back in high school when my classmates laughed at my super 8 movies. Would my script get produced and give me that thrill? I hoped so.

The first thing I did, when the script was still quite rough, was to enter it in a screenwriting contest. To my surprise and delight, the script passed one weeding-out round after another. The script ended up generating a lot of positive comments and winning semi-finalist honors.

I was confident that a more refined version of it would have a similar influence on production companies and agents. I mailed out scores of copies and then waited for the response. Some of it was very positive. I met with a number of executives, received some encouraging compliments, and was asked to pitch some other ideas. But ultimately, no one bit. Everyone liked the writing, but no

one thought they could make the script into a profitable movie. I disagreed, of course, but I had to face facts. I was a rookie writer with an offbeat script that would prove expensive to produce. No studio was going to gamble on me.

PLOT TWIST

It's a tough feeling to face this sort of rejection. I cursed myself for not writing something totally different—say, an easily explained thriller that could be filmed for peanuts. (And in fact I would advise all screenwriters to create a low-budget script when they're starting out—a lot more doors will open.) I knew that selling one's first script is the exception rather than the rule and that I shouldn't be disappointed, but I was nonetheless. When your vocation involves pulling lies out of thin air, it's very easy to lose confidence in your work. I had to convince myself that my stuff was good, but the more I worked for ICM, the more demoralized I became. I knew my work was better than most of the stuff I read. I felt that I cared more about movies than any of the agents, and yet I was still struggling. I caught myself complaining one day and I wondered, Am I being arrogant? The answer was yes. But the funny thing is, the arrogance felt good. It propelled me, made me want to create a body of work that no one could ignore.

Now, if I were an exemplary role model for achieving Hollywood success and this story had a wonderfully happy ending, I would tell you that I put my nose to the grindstone and monastically wrote until the studios drew blood in a bidding war for my screenplays. But in my experience, Hollywood doesn't work that way. To get work, to make a name for yourself, you squirm in any way you can, like a mobile, tenacious sperm. You must do anything to penetrate Hollywood success.

I put my screenplay aside for a while and wound up getting work as a researcher on a documentary. My diligence impressed the producer and he promised me future work associate producing documentaries for him. The money was decent, so I took work whenever I could get it. By day I worked my butt off as a producer and by night I wrote. In documentaries, the producer shapes the story like a writer does in features. You build the sequence; construct a beginning, middle, and end; determine what the characters are trying to do; and then judge the best way to depict all of these things so an audience will see things the way you do. Why, it's just like lying, only you're figuring out a way to tell the truth instead of falsehood.

Though I never gave up my dream to write screenplays, I came to enjoy the process of making documentaries. After my skills at producing documentaries impressed my boss, he gave me the chance to write one. Due to union rules, I couldn't receive on-screen credit for the half-hour show, but the feeling that something I had written had been produced was still deeply satisfying. It was around this time that my hard work began reaping rewards. I optioned my second screenplay and won a job writing and directing an hour-long documentary about dogs. The documentary turned out great and I'm currently working on my second draft of the optioned screenplay. Have I reached my goals yet? No, not by a long shot. I know it's going to take a lot more work and a lot more luck to become the filmmaker I want to be. But I feel I'm on the right track and in time I'll get there. And that's no lie.

Some Advice from Dave

Starting Out: First, get a life. That may sound like flip advice, but it's not meant to be. As a screenwriter, you'll be creating scenarios and writing dialogue for fictional characters that may be very different from you. Any time you spend with real-life characters who are different from you will help you get a handle on what you're writing. Travel, intern at a newspaper, volunteer, pour drinks. You'll be surprised by what you learn.

Know the Process: When you write a screenplay, you're creating a blueprint for a finished movie. And just as architects go to construction sites, screenwriters should know their way around a movie set. The more you know about how movies are made, the more you can ensure that your screenplays are filmed the way you intend. I highly recommend working as a production assistant on a feature-length movie.

Know Your Craft: This is the fun part: watch a ton of movies. If a movie really inspires you, watch it repeatedly. If you can, locate the script. The more attuned you are to the structure of motion pictures, the stronger your own structures will be. Seeing how other filmmakers resolve their impasses will help you resolve yours.

Educate Yourself: There are innumerable books available on screenwriting. My favorites are *Adventures in the Screen Trade* and *The Tools of Screenwriting* (see page 57). One of the best places in the world for plays and published screenplays is the Samuel French bookstores in Los Angeles and New York.

Location, Location, Location: Obviously, you can write screenplays any-where. You certainly don't have to pack up everything and go to Los Angeles to write. In fact, it can be intimidating to know that in any given L.A. grocery store, you're but one of dozens of screenwriters. Yet Los Angeles is definitely a company town, and if you want to be a part of the industry, you need to have some contact with it. Plus you can learn the business better there than anywhere else. If you're focused and energetic, you can find a movie industry job, keep abreast of what Hollywood is looking for, and make friends with writers and colleagues who will analyze your work.

What to Write: As a first-time writer, your best bet is to create something that's original, personal, and small in scope. Studios are far more likely to gamble on a new writer when the stakes are small. If your script is unique and can be filmed on a low budget, the odds are much better for getting a contract with a production company. If you want to direct as well, there's a much greater chance that you'll be allowed to do so if you've written a low-budget project.

Respect Your Field: Although screenplays are just the plans for a finished movie, they're still literature. Yet it's amazing how many amateur screen-writers disdain the art of writing. Script readers are a cynical bunch. If you give them a script full of misspellings, typos, and contradictions, they'll be against you from the start. After all, if you don't respect your work, why should anyone else?

Selling Yourself: When you're finished with your script, you have many choices. You can throw it back in the drawer and move on to your next one, produce it yourself, or start the submission process.

The Submission Process: Blind submissions to studios don't work. Instead start by obtaining a list of agents from the Writers Guild of America. Or read the motion picture trade magazines until you are familiar with the names of literary agents and the kind of writers they represent. Next, write a creative letter to as many as you can, telling them who you are, why your work is worthy of their attention, and why they should ask to see your script. More often than not, you'll get a response.

Surviving: If you're going to try your luck at this game, go in knowing that the odds are against you. Be prepared for rejection. It's not uncommon for writers to have six or seven unproduced spec scripts under their belts before they ink their first deal. It's even more likely that a writer will never sell anything. I'm not telling you not to try, but don't be unrealistic. Come here for the love of telling stories. If you're lucky, maybe, you'll also find someone who wants to listen to them.

A Few Resources to Help You Out

Adventures in the Screen Trade, by William Goldman (New York: Warner Books, 1983). An entertaining, though cautionary, look at a screenwriting career.

The Tools of Screenwriting, by David Howard and Edward Mabley (New York: St. Martin's Press, 1993). Highly recommended by people in the industry as one of the best guidebooks for writing a feature-length screenplay.

Variety (P.O. Box 6400, Torrance, Calif. 90504, [800] 323-4345). This trade journal provides the latest industry news along with listings of auditions, job openings, and new film releases.

Association of Independent Video and Film Makers, Foundation for Independent Video and Film (625 Broadway, Ninth Floor, New York, N.Y. 10012, [212] 473-3400). The AIVF publishes the *Independent Directory*, a guide that profiles independent film organizations. It also offers such services as group health care, a library of job and internship listings, trade discounts on equipment rentals, guest speakers from the industry, and ongoing network gatherings for members.

Getting Started in Film: The Official American Film Institute Guide to Exciting Film Careers, ed. Emily Laskin (New York: Prentice Hall, 1992). A collection of interviews with people who've made it in film. Producers, directors, cinematographers, actors, designers, and writers tell how they get started and offer good advice.

How to Be a Working Actor: The Insider's Guide to Finding Jobs in Theater, Film and Television, by Mari Lyn Henry and Lynne Rayas (New York: Backstage Books/Watson-Guptill Publications, 1994). This guide contains all of the specifics of preparing for and landing jobs as an actor, including advice on résumés, auditions, expenses, unions, regional markets, and more.

Stepping Onto the Corporate Ladder

Ever wonder what it would be like to throw yourself into a two-year stint on Wall Street? What if you joined a Fortune 500 firm after graduation? Or suppose you worked for an advertising agency, a small start-up company, a management consulting firm, or a publishing house—what would you experience then? Well, here's your chance to find out.

This section is written by graduates who were eager to move beyond abstract academic ideas and dive into bottom-line challenges. They are also people who, after years of scraping by as students, were ready to take home a steady paycheck and the financial security that comes with it.

Of course, if you have friends out in the working world, you may have already heard stories about starting out in business—cautionary tales about the long hours people work and the tedious tasks entry-level employees are expected to perform. The graduates in this section do have a few of these anecdotes to recount, but what's more engaging are the highlights they describe—being part of high-powered teams asked to solve challenging business problems, working with insightful supervisors, participating in client meetings and presentations, and being rewarded with increased responsibility and, perhaps, a promotion.

In the end, most entry-level business jobs are probably a combination of these two extremes. For every high-level presentation there are plenty of late nights spent in preparation. And for every intriguing business issue discussed there are usually many hours spent in front of a computer spreadsheet organizing the data. But as these essays reveal, starting out in business offers a tremendous opportunity to acquire experience and tangible skills. Whether you're in that high-level meeting or glued to your computer, there are subtle lessons to be learned every day—watching how one manager effectively encourages a coworker and how another's admonishments fail to inspire; taking a tip from a more senior employee on how to put together a persuasive report; or observing the way a successful superior treats her clients. As Rob Middleton, a Berkeley graduate who started out in advertising, puts it, "It's like learning a new language. When you're first starting a job you don't know anything about it, so you sponge up everything you experience."

Working on

Wall Street

Mark Gordon Silverman

The Wall Street investment bank analyst position—it's one of the most coveted jobs for college seniors seeking a career in business. According to Mark, plunging into this fast-paced, high-stakes world is certainly an intense educational experience. Drawing on his two-year stint as an analyst, he uses the following pages to demystify this illustrious position, describing its moments of glory along with its many hours of drudgery.

It's 6 A.M. and the Lincoln Town Car is late. When it finally arrives, I collapse in the backseat. The driver knows where to go. I look out the window at dawn breaking over New York City, a sight I've seen too often. While most people are sleeping, I'm just returning from work. Unlike a college all-nighter you can sleep off after the paper is turned in, when you work all night at an investment bank, you're still expected to be in the office by 8:30 that morning. Granted, all-nighters don't happen every day, but as I was told, "No one will feel bad if you're here till 1:00 A.M. every night. That's why we pay you the big bucks."

First Day

Four months after I walked off the graduation stage, I entered one of the countless skyscrapers that dot the landscape of Park Avenue and stepped off at the thirty-first floor. Fully armed with a new suit, a black leather briefcase, and a copy of the *Wall Street Journal*, I felt pretty good about life.

A receptionist greeted me and led me through an oak-paneled door. Already at this hour things were in full swing. From the main room I could see people darting down hallways, hurrying to offices, or having conferences on their phones. No one seemed to notice my entrance except a young woman, who introduced herself as Rhonda, my secretary.

Someone had thought of everything. In my desk drawers I found the equivalent of a small stationery store. Paper to post on walls, paper for the computer printer, corporate stationery, mailing labels—it seemed as though I was responsible for the destruction of a small rain forest.

On my desk sat an IBM computer. Little did I know that for the next two years, I would eat three meals a day in front of it. But not today. On my chair I found a memo welcoming me to the firm and inviting me to attend a small luncheon in my honor with other members of the firm, partners, vice presidents, and associates.

I passed my morning smiling and shaking hands. Every ten minutes someone would stop by my office and introduce him- or herself. Although their names and faces faded as they left the office, soon I would come to know them better than my own girlfriend. I would certainly spend more time with them in the wee hours of the morning than I would with her.

At 12:00 P.M. sharp, I was shown into the boardroom. Everything was just how you'd picture it. Dominating the room was a large oak table surrounded by twenty-four leather chairs. The walls were all paneled in wood. The food was excellent. So far being an invest-ment banker wasn't too bad.

After lunch, things changed. A vice president handed me a stack of ten annual reports and asked me to prepare an analysis by the morning. It was only as I was eating dinner in front of my computer, one quarter of the way through the stack, that I began to comprehend the magnitude of the task. At 2:00 A.M. I placed what I had done on his desk and ordered a car to take me home. The first day was over. The second was only a few hours away.

WHY WALL STREET?

It's funny, but I never really consciously asked myself, Why Wall Street? before I joined. Perhaps I didn't want to hear the answer. I had spent a tremendous amount of time preparing interview answers for why I wanted to work for blankety-blank bank, be it Goldman Sachs, Salomon Brothers, or Merrill Lynch, but I had never taken a step back and truly reflected on why I chose this field.

Thinking about it now, honestly, I'd have to say my primary motive was probably money. An analyst can expect to earn between $45,000 and $50,000 his or her first year, and that is just the beginning. I wanted not only the highest-paying job out of college but also the future that such a career guaranteed.

There is also a mystique associated with Wall Street that drew me in. Billion-dollar deals, power brokers deciding the financial fate of America, top-notch minds analyzing complex problems— the allure of this intense environment was hard to ignore.

WHAT DOES GORDON GECKO DO?

People who work on Wall Street pull on their suspenders and cinch up their ties each morning and race downtown to their high-powered offices, but once they're there, what exactly are they trying to achieve? It's a good question, and after hanging around for a couple of years, I think I have the basics down:

For starters, Wall Street banks have the critical responsibility of providing capital for corporations and for federal and municipal governments. If IBM wants to build a new manufacturing plant, it's likely to raise the money by issuing bonds (corporate debt) or offering more stock. Wall Street would be responsible for arranging this financing and finding people or organizations willing to buy the debt or stock. It would provide a similar service for a city that wants to finance a new sports stadium, or for the federal government if it needs funding for a foreign aid loan to Mexico or the development of a new satellite program.

Wall Street is not only responsible for the issuance of stocks and bonds, but it also manages the money for the people who buy them. A Wall Street bank will bring together people who have a common investing interest—biotech, China, high-risk start-up firms—and make investments for them. These banks, known as investment managers, buy stock in numerous companies reflecting that investing interest and watch over these investments for the investors. This is what mutual funds are all about.

Hostile takeovers, corporate raiders, junk bonds—Wall Street is probably best known for the lingo associated with mergers and acquisitions (M and A's). Every morning in the paper, you read about one company acquiring or making a bid for another company. Sometimes these takeovers are friendly and sometimes they are not. Investment banks are the ones that are behind the strategy and financing of these takeovers. When two companies decide to merge, an investment bank represents each side, negotiating on the corporation's behalf. When one company decides to take over another, investment banks make that happen, too. This work keeps many people busy all night long, including myself.

It's 4:00 a.m., I Must Be Doing an M and A

When I think of a financial analyst on Wall Street, I picture someone in a room with no windows, hunched over a computer, working on a spreadsheet into the wee hours of the morning. This basically was my life for two years.

As an analyst, one of your principle responsibilities is to do the number-crunching homework that every investment banking project requires. Say, for example, your bank has been hired by

two firms that are thinking of merging. You might be asked to create a financial model of what the merged company would look like. Very simply this means you would collect all of the information for both companies—the current market value of their real estate and manufacturing equipment, overhead costs, product inventory—put it into spreadsheets, and then develop a way to combine them (a very tedious and time-consuming process). All of this scrambling lays the groundwork for your bank's ultimate goal—evaluating whether this merger is a good idea and deciding what price should be paid for the company that is being taken over.

Analysts also get to play private investigator, learning as much as they can about how a client may stand up against its competitors. I'll never forget one project in which the chairman of the board of a very large bank in the Midwest wanted us to help him decide what to do with his corporation. Should it be merged with another company, sold outright, restructured, or simply dissolved? To be able to answer those questions, we needed to know everything we could about the situation. I spent six weeks working until 3:00 A.M. every night gathering data. I felt like Radar O'Reilly on "M.A.S.H." going to the ends of the earth to find whatever we needed. Some days I was at the New York Public Library compiling Federal Reserve data. Other times I was calling up the bank's competitors for information not included in the annual reports, often posing as an investor. Then I'd be making calls to the state where the bank was located, gleaning whatever I could about the cities where there were branches. If the data existed, I would find it.

What does it take to succeed as an analyst? Analytical skills certainly help in the realm of spreadsheets and stock evaluation. Investigative ingenuity serves you well for data collection. However, the most critical, and least glamorous, talent needed to be a good analyst is the ability to do "due diligence"—to pay attention to the meticulous details. This was often my primary role on projects. If my firm was creating a new mutual fund, I was the one assigned to work with the lawyers who were writing the prospectus, the legal document that describes the investment. By the time it went out, I would have reread the document fifty times for typos, misspellings, anything at all that would reflect poorly on our professionalism and competence. When we developed marketing materials to sell this fund to potential investors, yours truly would take it to the printer, oversee the typesetting, and hit the print button. When we needed to file forms with the Securities and Exchange Commission and Standard and Poors about the fund, I would be the one who walked around the office pestering people for their signature.

PLAYERS WITH NO TIME TO PLAY

There are some analysts on Wall Street who call themselves players. They like to think of themselves as high-powered professionals in a high-powered field. Maybe someday they will be, but right now they are simply the lowest guys on the totem pole. That's the way it is in this business, and playing the role requires paying some heavy dues.

I don't think I made plans with friends during the entire two years I was on Wall Street, because inevitably they would have had to have been canceled. Going out during the week was unheard of. All I ever wanted to do on the weekend was sleep. In fact, my girlfriend began to think of me as more of an acquaintance, and decided to find a new boyfriend. Such are the sacrifices for success.

As warped as this lifestyle may sound, it wouldn't be so bad if you were actually working all the time. But much of your efforts as an analyst are invested in "face time." If an associate or vice president you are working for is still at the office at 9:00 P.M., you will be too, even if you have nothing to do. That associate may drop off work for you on his way out at eleven, but in the interim, you will twiddle your thumbs. There's no reason why you shouldn't be able to spend those precious two hours at a café with a friend, but of course this wouldn't get you very far in the corporate world.

ROLLERBLADING TOWARD THE FINISH LINE

For me, the strain of investment banking began to take its toll. Quite simply, by my second year, I was burned out. The highlight of my workday came during the morning commute, as I Rollerbladed down Fifty-Second Street with my tie flying behind me. Once I arrived in the office, the fun was over.

I had mixed feelings as my two-year stint came to a close. I had learned a tremendous amount and acquired some very valuable skills. At the same time, I couldn't wait to leave. I looked forward to hanging out with friends, dating, and just plain sleeping.

As I packed my belongings, I took an oblong glass paperweight off my desk. Inside it was a check for $1,228,500,000.00. It wasn't issued to me, of course, since it would have taken me 24,570 years to earn that. This trophy was the money used to establish the largest bond fund our firm had ever put together. It also represented the many late nights I spent hunched over a computer helping to make it happen.

Now that check sits on my bookshelf just above my Rollerblades. Every now and then I take it down and reflect on the high-rolling game I briefly played on Wall Street. I do not regret how I spent those years. I would do it all over again. I would not, however, spend the next two years that way.

Some Advice from Mark

Knowing What You Want: There are several investment banking departments that recruit on college campuses—corporate finance, sales and trading, and research. Before you go through the interview process, it's important to know which department you are interested in. Do your homework: read up on literature in your college career center and call recent alumni in the industry.

Interviewing: Investment banks are notorious for asking questions that require you to think on your feet. Before your interviews, hold practice sessions with friends.

Why Our Firm?: Wall Street firms are all cut from the same cloth, but each likes to view itself as a unique club with a certain culture. They will inevitably ask, "Why our firm?" You should have an answer. Also, make sure you know as much as you can about the firm's recent business—look for newspaper articles and do research at the library.

Annual Reports: Reading the investment banks' annual reports can provide some useful tidbits for your interviews. Since almost all of the big investment banks are public companies, you should be able to get your hands on these documents. If your career center doesn't already carry them, call up the investor relations department for each firm and ask for a copy.

Summer Internship: If possible, try to find an internship during college. Firms make a huge investment in training graduates after college. If you have already proven yourself, you will be much less of a risk to them.

Study Spreadsheets: Know how to use the Excel and Lotus 1-2-3 spreadsheet programs. If you seek a career in investment banking, they will shortly become your best friends. A proven ability to use them can only make you a more attractive candidate.

A Few Resources to Help You Out

The Corporate Finance Sourcebook (New York: McGraw Hill, 1994). Unless you're already an investment banker, you're not going to want to shell out the big bucks to buy this book, but it is worth reviewing at the library. It contains an extensive listing of companies in the various subfields of finance—real estate, investment banking, venture capital, and so on.

Nelson Directory of Investment Managers (Portchester, N.Y.: Nelson Publications, 1995). A handy reference you may find at the library. This guide contains data on a myriad of investment organizations. It includes contact names and financial information. Although published to serve investors, it's equally useful for motivated job seekers.

Liar's Poker, by Michael Lewis (New York: Penguin Books, 1990). "If you want to know what really happens on Wall Street, and to have a good laugh in the process, you ought to read *Liar's Poker*," says *Newsday*.

Barbarians at the Gate: The Fall of RJR Nabisco, by Bryan Burroughs (New York: HarperPerennial/HarperCollins, 1990). A fascinating account of the largest takeover in Wall Street history.

Finding Big

Business

in a Small

Company

Amy Dalton

With corporate America doing more firing than hiring, many graduates are deciding to look for jobs elsewhere. One of the fastest-
growing alternatives is small- and medium-size businesses. In this
essay, Amy draws on her experience with a small publishing company to highlight some of the advantages and disadvantages such
jobs have to offer.

"So, what are you going to do with that?"

This was the standard, baffled response whenever I told people
my major. No, that's not quite right. First came the blank stare.
Then I had to explain: "Well, American studies is an interdisciplin-
ary major embracing history, literature, sociology, political science,
and art."

You could just see the wheels turning in their heads. They were
doing the math. "Let's see. Four years in college at a jillion dollars
a year, and now the girl thinks that she can get a job with *that*?
What a waste of cash."

I knew what they were thinking, and to be honest, I was just as
worried as they were. Of course, I'd never show it. A little defiantly,
I would reply, "Well, um, I could do anything."

But that was just it. What would that "anything" be? My extremely mediocre performance in computer science indicated that a bright future in Silicon Valley wasn't very likely. I also knew, after tottering on high heels to the Career Planning and Placement Center for endless interviews with companies that wouldn't hire me because I hadn't taken econ (but I didn't *like* econ, you see), that my glorious career as an investment banker was sadly not to be.

Nevertheless, I had to find something. I eventually decided to focus on one of the things I did best—babbling. Having churned out countless papers on subjects ranging from Hemingway's portrayal of women to the golden age of American industrialism to the social ramifications of alarm clock snooze bars, I figured there must be some way to turn that ability to wax eloquent about anything into a paying vocation. When graduation rudely pushed me into the real world, I made up my mind—public relations, advertising, or publishing was to be my calling.

Unfortunately, at that time, positions in PR and advertising were few and far between. Trying to be positive about it, I figured that that simply made my search easier. I answered any ad that had the word *publishing* in it, fantasizing about glamour, intelligentsia, and long, heartfelt lunches with Barbara Kingsolver. Finally, in February, my quest came to a successful end when I landed a real job in publishing. The only problem was that it wasn't exactly the big-time publisher I had envisioned.

STARTING SMALL

The company that hired me was a small publishing company that specialized in high-priced newsletters and conferences, catering to the public relations industry. I discovered very quickly that the glamour, fame, and large paychecks were a long way off—Barbara would just have to wait. Like any recent graduate trying to break into publishing, I started out at the very bottom, making a whopping $18,000 a year as a publisher's assistant.

It also didn't take me long to realize that working at a small company was going to be a little different. To begin with, I could forget about posh offices, modern furniture, and panoramic downtown views. Starting small meant starting simple. My day started with a bus ride through scary parts of town to the office, which was in a shabby warehouse across the street from a sake factory. And my office . . . well, it wasn't exactly an office. Believe it or not, I sat at a secondhand desk perched in a hallway at the top of some stairs. I felt a little like the gatekeeper without a keymaster.

Not having a real office, however, didn't keep me from having real work. My next discovery was that having a job in a small company actually means having eight million jobs crammed into one. As is the case in many organizations that have a large workload and not much money, I was expected to play multiple roles. I started by spending half of my time working for the publisher as his glorified secretary. I did his filing, made his hair appointments and tennis court reservations, proofed his copywriting projects, and fetched his coffee. (Actually, I had to go down the street every week or so to get coffee for the entire company. Just between you and me, I started drinking tea as my silent protest.)

The other half of my time was spent working for the product manager for the media newsletters and conferences. I handled all of the registrations for the conferences, helped research and invite speakers, ran up and down those damn stairs to the art department and print shop to make sure the marketing materials were on schedule. Between the two jobs, I became somewhat of a jack-of-all-trades, doing any bizarre task thrown my way, learning a little about a lot of different parts of the business.

GROWING IN OFFICE

You're still reading? Well, I'm glad you haven't given up on small-business experience, because along with the hallway offices and menial duties there are some potential perks. One of the most tantalizing is the opportunity to quickly take on greater responsibil-

ity. In a small office you don't have the rigid hierarchy and elaborate hiring protocol of a large corporation, so one change in the staff can be a big opportunity for someone at the bottom. It was for me. Less than a year after I started, the product manager announced that he was leaving to go to graduate school. After a transition period in which it seemed like we were all passengers in a speeding car with no one watching the road, I was promoted to product manager. I earned more money, gained more responsibility, and got an office (with a door).

For someone who didn't even take econ, I was amazed to find myself—literally—the business manager of my own little publishing empire. After an afternoon crash course in Lotus 1-2-3, I learned how to analyze complex direct-mail campaigns and make recommendations for new ones. I learned how to manage three editors, an art department, a customer service department, a print shop, and a mail room to make sure that every month, without fail, six newsletters landed securely on subscribers' desks. I launched my own newsletter. I learned how to call up the technology editors for *Forbes* and *Fortune* to invite them to speak at conferences. I learned how to handle editors who attempted to use the conference as a soap box to scream at public relations executives—who had kindly paid me $350 for the privilege. I wrote monthly reports on the status of the products based on stacks of financial statements. I learned how to negotiate contracts with hotels and choose lunch menus for three hundred. And I learned how to create a budget and marketing plan for a multimillion-dollar product cluster.

Being part of a small organization, especially a small publisher, it wasn't hard to find tangible results for my efforts. You can see the subscriber numbers climb, you can see the finished product go out the door, you can count the checks coming in, you can talk to the people attending your conferences, you can see your ideas implemented every day. You make a difference.

RISKY BUSINESS

There was, however, a flip side to this. When you're part of a small firm, there's not a lot of room for slack. If you don't get your work done, no one else is going to do it for you. That meant spending plenty of late lights and weekends at the office. Another drawback to working for a small business is that no matter what "they" tell you, small companies are financially unstable institutions with very little long-term security. During my two years at this company, we went through four accountants that I remember. It was always a struggle to make payroll—not something to joke about when you're living paycheck to paycheck. We were forever fending off irate vendors. On more than one occasion, I almost came to blows with the publisher over why, even though we had just made a $50,000 profit on a conference, we didn't have a dime to pay the hotel bill. I learned the hard way that when every penny counts, your mistakes make a much bigger fiscal splash in a small pond than they do in the ocean of a multinational corporation. I found this constant worry over finances very stressful.

It's a Small World After All

There are thousands of students in business schools all over the country pouring over case studies, developing elaborate models for increasing market share, and surveying thousands of customers. But in my opinion, business comes down to two things: personalities and relationships. As students, it's easy to take relationships for granted. You have your friends, and then there's everybody else. If you don't like a professor, you don't have to take another class with him or her. Better yet, drop the class!

Yet in a small business, relationships can make the average work-day a heaven on earth or a living hell. Too bad if the computer guy is an irascible grump, you just lost your C drive with six months' worth of work and you need his help to duct tape your machine back together. You know that the fulfillment director will blow a gasket if you tell him he gave you the wrong report, but you need his report to write yours. You know the accountant is going to get fired tomorrow, but you still need him to cut you a check today. Your boss's wife is also the art director and you find yourself acting as negotiator between them on whose turn it is to pick the kids up from school—meanwhile, FedEx won't wait.

But the most important relationship of all is your relationship with the owner. It's one thing to work in a large corporation with armies of employees—if you don't get along with your manager, you have alternatives; you can go to the human resources depart-ment or talk to your boss's boss. In a small business, the personality of the owner sets the tone for the whole corporate culture; if you don't get along with the owner, you're sunk.

Even if you do get along with everyone, some aspects of working in a small business can be so subtle that they take you by surprise. After spending most of my life in schools surrounded by friends all day and night, I suddenly found myself isolated, working in a random warehouse with the same handful of people day in and day out. As it happened in my case, everyone was at least five to twenty years older than me. I consider myself lucky to have made a few solid friendships, but I missed the easy camaraderie of my peers.

TAKING A STEP BACK

There's no question that working for a small company has its frustrating moments. Compact quarters, quarrelsome coworkers, and heavy workloads can make graduate school begin to look very attractive.

During the difficult times, I would always try to remind myself that it was *because* of the challenges of working in a small company that I was benefiting so much from the experience. When you think about it, where else was I going to double my salary in two years? Where else was I going to be catapulted into a managerial position, entrusted with millions of dollars, in a matter of months? How else was I going to become an effective, compassionate supervisor? How else was a liberal arts major (without even the hint of an econ class on my transcript) going to go from schlepping coffee to running a business? How else was I going to learn how to stand up for myself in the big, bad corporate world? How else could I learn to think creatively on my feet, because it's expected of me? And where else was I going to do this by the time I was twenty-five?

Looking back, I realize that I have now what I didn't have before I worked at a small company: experience. It's that infuriating catch-22 of the working world. You can't get experience without experience. One way for getting real, hands-on business savvy is with a small, growing company in a field that interests you. In a small company, that entry-level job you gambled on can suddenly turn into a prestigious career. You might start out in the hallway like I did, but in a small company, chances are you won't be there for long. The opportunities are yours for the taking.

With a sigh of relief and a little smile, I think about the people who thought I wouldn't make it in the working world with a liberal arts degree. With a little less defiance and a little more confidence, I say to them, "I could do anything now."

Some Advice from Amy

The Needle in the Haystack: Finding the small company that will give you a big break is half the challenge. Don't underestimate your local want ads, word of mouth, or friends of your parents. Other options are job banks and alumni networks. Companies can list jobs at these places for free, and it's a good way to network informally with people looking for the same kind of jobs you are. If you know what industry you're interested in, you'll find newsletters and publications that service those industries are a great source for opportunities—whether it's a job listing or an article about a company you might want to send your résumé to for an informational interview. Luck is also a factor, so cut yourself some slack and allow time for all of this to happen.

Don't Let the Revolving Door Hit You in the Butt: When you're interviewing, find out how long people have been with the company. If most employees have worked there for three or more years, that's a good sign that the company is stable and the people enjoy their jobs. If you find that most of the employees have been around less than six months, this might be a sign of widespread burnout, a bad working environment, disorganization, or, alternatively, rapid growth. Also, find out from more senior employees if they feel they're still growing in their careers. Just treading water in the same, boring job might be the last thing you want when you're just starting out.

What's the Bottom Line? Before you accept a job with any company, especially a small one, it is within your right to be honestly informed about its financial situation. It is understandable that a growing company might not have a tight grip on cash flow, and all companies hit rough spots, but if the ship is about to sink, you could find yourself looking for another job a lot sooner than you planned.

Get Your Piece of the Pie: An advantage of working in a small business is that if you contribute to its profit, it is more than happy to reward you. Most large corporations have a set percentage for raises and a rigid structure for promotions. If you work in a small firm, however, you can sit down with the owner or your immediate boss and carve out a bonus plan. The concept is simple: if you make them money, you make money. This could turn out to mean thousands of dollars in your pocket and financial success for your firm.

Be a Renaissance Man (or Woman): When you're interviewing with a small business, emphasize your willingness to try anything, take risks, accept responsibility, and successfully juggle many different tasks at once. Back it up with examples from your life, but keep in mind that they need not be work-related experiences—school, family, friends, and your part-time delivery job for the local pizza joint all qualify.

I Think I'll Be a . . . (Fill in the Blank): You know better than anyone what you like to do. Unlike a corporation that hires people for specific, defined jobs, in a small company you have the latitude to create your own job description. While you may be the "assistant," what you do has less to do with your official title than with your strengths and interests.

Independence Is a Virtue: One thing people in a small business don't have a lot of is time. Every hour that you work is an hour that your boss doesn't have to put in overtime. You will be the hero of the office if people know they can delegate work to you and you will get the job done with minimal hand-holding.

Toto, We're Not in Kansas Anymore: Think about where this job will take you two years, five years, ten years down the yellow brick road. Will you obtain the skills you want to launch yourself in the career you've chosen? Or, if you don't have any idea where you're headed, will this company reveal unknown opportunities?

It Ain't Over Till It's Over: Don't underestimate the influence your small company can have on your future career. Your company might be small potatoes now, but the owner of your company might help you get a job with the industry leader. If you're interested in graduate school, your experiences and the recommendations of your employer could put you over the top.

A Few Resources to Help You Out

A Big Splash in a Small Pond: Finding a Great Job in a Small Company, by R. Linda Resnick with Kerry H. Pechter (New York: Simon and Schuster, 1994). A useful research tool for tracking down small companies in your field of choice. It also has good suggestions on how to get hired.

Local business papers. According to *A Big Splash in a Small Pond*, regional business papers often publish a list of the one hundred fastest-growing small companies in their area. Local business directories and your chamber of commerce may offer leads as well.

Business America On-Line ([402] 593-4503). A commercial on-line service that contains hundreds of thousands of businesses indexed by industry, number of employees, rate of growth, and location. One of the best sources for job searchers is the file of twelve thousand companies with annual growth of 20 percent or more.

Forbes "Up-and-Comers: The 200 Best Small Companies in America" (Forbes Inc., 60 Fifth Avenue, New York, N.Y. 10011, [212] 620-2200). Every November, *Forbes* magazine lists the two hundred fastest-growing small companies. Look for back copies in the library or call Forbes.

Playing the

Advertising

Game

Kristine Molander

Advertising is a casual, creative industry that has strong bottom-line goals. Kristine found this dynamic field to be the perfect place to combine her business acumen and her interest in communication. In this essay she shares what she's learned since joining the game.

Advertising lured me in with its catchy jingles, its excitement, its humor, its responsiveness, and its controversial ability to alter the way we live our lives. Let's face it, how many of us closet NBA wanna-bes *really* buy our Air Jordans for their superior maneuverability and triple cushion features? Come on, be honest. For people like me, at least, it's a commercial-driven urge to Just Do It and Be Like Mike.

It's no big surprise, really, that commercials have such a strong influence on our lives. Those of us leaving college today are part of a generation that grew up in front of the tube. If life imitates art, then our lives are a medley of seventies sitcoms—a demented amalgamation of Marcia Brady, Jeannie, Danny Partridge, and Gilligan and the Skipper, too. Imagine a middle-aged corporate exec trying to target his products at our generation. Unless he understands where we're coming from, he won't stand a chance.

This challenge is part of what drew me to advertising. If you're working for an advertising agency, the onus is on you to educate your clients on how to use media to best position their products for continued growth. Or, in English, it is your job to figure out how to actually reach the twenty-something generation and whatever other audience your clients want to target. The entire advertising process combines a fascinating look at the psychological and economical impact of human behavior—what drives us, motivates us, inspires us, and even aggravates us can all influence product supply and demand. Advertising is immediate, up front and personal, creative, and extremely fast paced. It has to be, otherwise it wouldn't be able to keep up with the TV generation and the rest of the ever-changing global marketplace.

Qualifying for the Game

These are the motivating factors that encouraged me to seek an on-campus interview with Leo Burnett, U.S.A, one of the largest advertising agencies in the United States. They are also the reason I was so elated when I actually got the interview, that is, until I started talking to other people. Let's just say people who had interviewed with various agencies did not have the most flattering stories to tell. In fact, the tales became taller and scarier with each person.

"Watch out! They'll ask you to name what kitchen utensil you'd most like to be and why."

"Yeah, I once had an interviewer who turned his back on me and didn't say anything for the entire interview."

"Oh yeah? Well, one woman asked me to revitalize a whole line of gardening tools with one statement . . . and *then* back it up with an entire creative strategy, complete with storyboards for commercials, brand slogans, and . . . blah, blah, blah."

To the disappointment of my melodramatic friends, however, my interview was hardly a horror story. While I was looking forward to making a clever retort to the kitchen utensil question, all I really talked about with my interviewer was my family background (I

come from a family of eleven, and I use this in all of my interviews because it's a bit unusual), several on-campus achievements, and Leo Burnett's impressive client list.

I did heed one very helpful piece of advice from a friend, though: I got a copy of the agency's client list from the campus career library and read a few issues of *Ad Age* to bring myself up to speed on some of its clients' brands (how McDonald's was planning to introduce its latest McSomething, what United Airlines' new pricing strategy would be, why Tony the Tiger was such a hit for Kellogg's). As a result, I had something to say when the interviewer asked me what audience I thought Pillsbury was trying to target by buying airtime during a certain block of programs.

Apparently, doing my homework paid off, because I made it to the next round of play—an office interview visit, red-carpet treatment and all. I was wined, dined, and given a hotel suite with a bathroom bigger than my campus apartment living room (and it had a phone!). As someone who had had to share a room with her twin sister most of her life, I was quite impressed. After a whirlwind round of six interviews with six *very* different people (which I thought was a good sign) and a few weeks to think about all the things I should have brought up or not said at all, I was offered a chance to join the team as a media buyer/planner.

THE PLAYERS

At an advertising agency there are three different branches: creative, media, and account management. The creative department is where the writers and art directors (who get to wear jeans and T-shirts every day and have offices filled with romper room toys) conceptualize and design the ads. The client—McDonald's or Pillsbury—will give them information about a product and the creative team is supposed to come up with a compelling way to sell it. It's a glamour job, but it can also be grueling, considering that being creative on cue is not always an easy thing to do.

The media department, where I started, is responsible for making sure the message the creative team has designed reaches the right audience. Working within a specific budget, we develop a media strategy that will enable us to reach the target audience with enough frequency to have an impact. After all, the creative message won't do your client any good if no one in the target audience sees it—or worse, if you pay money for the wrong audience to see it.

Account management is comprised of a team of mediators who run between the client, creatives, media, and other departments, trying to keep everyone happy and making sure the advertisement actually goes all the way from concept to reality. It's part business, part juggling, and part marriage counseling.

LEARNING THE RULES AND PICKING TEAMS

One of the advantages of working for a large agency is that they usually explain the rules of the game before they ask you to pick up the ball and run with it. At Leo Burnett, that meant twenty colleagues, and I had the chance to go through a complete classroom training in all areas of the media management process—media research, negotiation, spreadsheet analysis. It was a chance for us to acquire tangible job skills and for our supervisors to observe where each of our strengths lay.

Sometime near the end of training, the moment arrives when you're assigned an account. You may have known nothing about Clorox cleaning products before you were hired, but if that's your account, you will soon. Or perhaps it will be Honey Nut Cheerios, Black & Decker tools, or Kodak film. If you're lucky, it may be a product or service that's targeted at young adults—Levi's, Nike, Miller Lite. If you're not so lucky, you may end up learning more than you ever wanted to know about Geritol or Depends. In my case, Virginia Slims was to become my speciality.

PLAY BALL!

Once you have gone through the interviews and training and have been assigned to an account team, what is it exactly that you do?

As a media planner, your job is to work with the account and creative groups to understand your brand's overall strategy and then come up with specific media goals to meet that strategy. For example, if the Virginia Slims brand team wanted to project a more contemporary, social image, it would be my job to try to suggest the most effective ways of using different types of media to accomplish that goal.

This is all done through a "media plan," which is basically a huge compilation of facts about who buys a product and how you can reach them—which television programs they're most likely to watch, which magazines they read, which movies they see, where they buy their groceries. For the Virginia Slims account, for example, I might develop a media plan that would target women between the ages of twenty-five and forty-nine who smoke. I would begin my research by finding out what the other cigarette brands were doing (where did our competition spend their media dollars last year?), paying particular attention to women's brands. Next it would be my job to develop criteria for evaluating different potential media sources. Factors might include cost efficiency, percentage of smokers in the audience, and total audience size. Using these criteria, I would rank the different types of media and come up with a list of key media vehicles I felt we should use in our plan.

Fourteen pencils and three hundred pages later, I would take the plan to my supervisor, and together we would evaluate the work and make adjustments. Finally, after examining all of the information we gathered, it would be my job to actually lay out our vision for which types of media our client should use and when they should be used. Then we would be off to the client to actually present our findings and hope the plan is approved.

KEEPING SCORE

Like most fast-paced businesses, advertising has its challenges. There seems to be a never-ending stream of deadlines to be met, and as each deadline approaches, my workday inevitably becomes longer and longer. But at the same time, I know I'm benefiting from the experience. It's kind of like being a rubber band—I feel my associates stretch my imagination, logic, and decision-making skills to the point where I really am intellectually challenged. This, coupled with the excitement of being an integral part of a project from beginning to end, is what keeps me going until three in the morning, putting finishing touches on a client presentation or making those last-minute revisions the client needs in a New York minute. Of course the business lunches, cross-country client meetings, top-of-the-line computers and resources, plus company funding for graduate school help, too. Plus, as you can imagine, working in a creative field is energizing, upbeat, and fun.

After spending two years at Leo Burnett, I'm still playing the game, but I've changed teams. (In the ad world, the most common way to increase your marketability and earning potential is to change companies.) At my new, smaller firm, I'm constantly utilizing the business acumen and political protocol I learned at Leo Burnett to function effectively in a capricious advertising environment. Looking back at the contacts I made, the credibility I built, and the experience I gained in the past two years, I am happy with the script I chose for life after college.

Some Advice from Kristine

Informational Interviews: I can't emphasize enough how important these are. Advertising companies hire based on their immediate needs. Because they rarely have vacant positions, setting up as many informational interviews as possible will get your foot in the door. That way, when a position does open up, you're more than just one more page in a stack of résumés.

Résumés: Because advertising is a creative field, having an unusual or unique résumé, if done well, can really help your cause. I had one friend, for example, who landed a job by creating a résumé that read like a personals ad.

Interviewing: Before you go in, know what your favorite ads are and be able to give compelling reasons for why you think they are effective. It doesn't hurt to choose an ad that the agency you are interviewing with has produced.

Internships: If you're still in school, a part-time internship one or two days a week is a great way to get a step up. Even if it's not in the department or company you want to be in, just having work experience is a real asset. Anything that's business related will give you greater credibility.

Big Versus Small Companies: It really depends on what your specific needs are. In general, a smaller company can offer a more hands-on approach to working, a quicker track to management, and less bureaucracy. A big company, on the other hand, can offer a more professional environment, better benefits and training, a stronger reputation, and a multitude of different people to work with.

Making Contact: Having just one contact in the industry can be extremely useful. Definitely take advantage of the young alumni from your school who have gone into the industry. Most recent graduates are sympathetic and willing to help others out.

A Few Resources to Help You Out

Getting Into Advertising, by David Laskin (New York: Ballantine Books, 1986). The book that ad agencies recommend most to interested job seekers. In addition to practical how-to advice about breaking into advertising, it has detailed job descriptions, interviews with people in the industry, and listings of addresses and phone numbers for the top agencies.

American Association of Advertising Agencies (666 Third Avenue, New York, N.Y. 10017). This is the best-known association of advertising agencies. You can contact 4A for a free listing of names and addresses of its members. For a fee of two dollars, you can also receive a twenty-page booklet called *Go for It: A Guide to Careers in Advertising*, which describes different jobs in advertising and advice about how to get in.

American Advertising Federation, Educational Services (1101 Vermont Avenue NW, Suite 500, Washington, D.C. 20005). For ten dollars, this organization will provide a listing of all of the advertising internships available at U.S. agencies.

Standard Directory of Advertising Agencies (Wilmette, Ill.: Reed Reference Publishing). Known by everyone in the industry as the "Agency Redbook," this is the bible of the advertising profession. It contains information about almost every advertising agency in the country. You can find it at your local library.

Advertising Age (Crain Communications, 220 East Forty-second Street, New York, N.Y. 10017, [212] 210-0725). Recent graduates say that anyone interested in getting into advertising must read this weekly trade magazine. Essential for job hunters are the special issues on America's leading agencies (spring), the top one hundred national advertisers (fall), and leading media companies (summer). Most libraries carry it.

Advertising Week (A/S/M Communications, 49 East Twenty-first Street, New York, N.Y. 10010, [212] 529-5500). This too is a must-read journal, according to people in the industry. Again, it should be in the library.

Starting Out

in Sales

David Rabkin

With little or no business experience, it's often difficult for recent grads to find a way into downsizing corporate America. Starting out in sales, however, is one path that has given some grads a way to get a foot in the door. That's exactly what David tried, and in this essay, he describes the ups and downs he encountered along the way.

"You won't be in sales forever," I was told during my interview. "We would be hiring you with the expectation that you would move up quickly." These words were still ringing in my ears as I surveyed my new surroundings. After three days of one-on-one training in the office and three more in the field, this was the beginning of my first day on the job. At 7:00 A.M. I was wading through the crowded back room of a San Francisco grocery store looking for that one case of Procter & Gamble Tide with Bleach.

I don't think I'll ever be able to decide which was most daunting: the industrial sinks full of rotting lettuce, the endless mountains of products to hunt through, or the walk-in freezers the size of my apartment I had to stand inside to count inventory.

Fortunately, I still had that first-day-on-the-job zeal, so by 7:45

I managed to finish my search and was ready for my next task—restocking our products on the shelf. I loaded cases of Folgers, Pampers, and Palmolive on a dolly and headed for the coffee section, and in no time had the shelves empty and the aisle filled with coffee cans. That's when the manager arrived and demanded to know what I was doing.

"Well ... I ... uh ... I'm supposed to fix it ..."

"Never touch the shelves without asking me first!"

"I'm sorry, I'm from Procter and Gamble ..."

"Oh, you guys. Well, try not to make a mess, and tell me when you're done."

An hour later my dolly was empty and the shelves were full. Now, finally, I was ready to do what I came for: sell. With one more mental walk-through of my objectives, I set out to find the manager again. I spotted him across the deli counter and cut him off in the seafood department.

"I have three display ideas for you today," I said, half out of breath. "I'll only take about five minutes of your time. My first idea is—"

"I don't have five minutes today. You'll have to come back later."

As the manager disappeared behind the beer display, I realized I had arrived. This was the big time. I was a sales representative. I had eagerly believed the words of corporate recruiters and embarked upon a career in management at a Fortune 500 company.

———————

When I began my senior year in college, I knew little more than that I wanted to be featured in a *Fortune* magazine article. I read about CEOs and Wall Street hotshots and thought, A business career is the thing for me. How I was supposed to go from a bachelor's degree in English to the cover of *Business Week*, however, was less than obvious.

Like any confused soon-to-be graduate, I started asking questions. I asked everybody I knew, and some people I didn't, about how I should get into business. The more I asked, the more I kept hearing a few big names—General Electric, AT&T, Clorox, and

Procter & Gamble. The reason: these corporate giants were known for strong training programs and a good introduction into the corporate world. For someone who didn't already possess a lot of practical skills, getting that kind of structured experience made a lot of sense. So that's where I stopped looking.

Satisfied with this summation of my career needs, I flipped open the schedule of on-campus recruiting interviews and circled the job interviews that fit the bill. I quickly realized that with an undergraduate degree in a nontechnical major, I would have to hang my hat on sales management as my foot in the door with all of the big names. While the "sales" part didn't particularly appeal to me, there was that "M" word after it, and that made my mouth water.

In a nutshell, that's how I found myself in the back room of that first grocery store at the crack of dawn. The whole time I was weighing my career options, I never really considered what my life would be like as a salesperson. Looking back on what I've gained from the experience, I don't regret the choice I made. Still, it would have been nice to know a little bit more ahead of time. So for those of you who are still figuring things out, let me share a little bit more about my experience.

The Home Office

For many sales reps in the corporate world, your work is done on the road—you might be traveling to medical offices to discuss pharmaceutical products, visiting businesses to sell computer hardware, or driving from store to store in search of shelf space for your grocery products. Whatever type of sales calls you make, you probably won't actually be spending much time in your office. For me, that was a tough adjustment. Before starting, I had envisioned being around many other interesting young people. What I soon found out was that my home base was just that: my home.

There are some advantages to the home office—I can have lunch whenever and as many times as I want each day, for example. More luxuriously, if I decide to start as early as, say, 5:00

A.M., I can be done with my job by 3:00. This flexibility, however, comes at a significant cost: the stress of my job is with me twenty-four hours a day. With an office job, you can leave some of that stress behind when you walk out the door. Whether you leave at five o'clock or ten, you can always go home. Working at home means you are never truly away from your work. When I wake up in the morning, and, likewise, when I go to sleep at night, I see my "office" at the foot of my bed. The night before a big presentation, I might wake up at 2:30 A.M. to change a comma or switch the order of two pages.

SALES MANAGEMENT

What do I do each day as a sales rep? That's the question I failed to ask going in, so I want to do my best to answer it for you. Aside from meetings, training, and about a half day's worth of paperwork every two weeks, I used to spend my days going in and out of grocery stores, following the scenario of my first day on the job. Of course, things did get better. After two years in the stores, I now spend most of my time discussing promotions and in-store merchandising ideas with store managers, and very little time actually moving boxes of products. As my store procedures became more efficient and my plans were set in motion, I had more time to think of new ideas and had gained the confidence of my customers, who allowed me to try them out in their stores.

No matter how well I got to know my customers, though, I always felt a twinge of nervousness before a presentation. Selling requires the ability to approach a person who holds an organization's decision-making power, look them straight in the eye, and tell them they are wrong. To sell requires confidence bordering on arrogance and a quick response for every objection. For some, these skills are innate, but if you've ever watched a little baby, you know that the square peg can also be squeezed into the round hole. I was one of the babies given the wrong peg and I had to push and push until my skills fit into the sales mold I was given. Sales managers expect their people to deliver results, which means that I am expected to convince my customers to buy as much of my company's product as possible. My biggest hurdle was coming to terms with the fact that on a routine basis, I had to push and cajole my customers into making decisions they would probably have put off, albeit to our mutual detriment. As a salesperson I am not always popular, and when things go wrong, I am blamed, not only by my superiors but also by the people to whom I sell.

As tough as this job can be, however, or perhaps because of it, I have experienced few things more satisfying than walking into a grocery store that sells a million dollars' worth of groceries a week and seeing the entire front lobby filled with my products. At times like those, my mind would wander to the thousands of customers who would soon walk by that display, do a double take, and then purchase my company's product when they otherwise might have purchased a competitor's. My work may not be earth-shattering, but it touches nearly everybody's life in some way.

DID I DO THE RIGHT THING?

Looking back on it, I have to ask myself if it was all worthwhile. I can act sentimental about the contribution I made to society, but I know that many other jobs provide a far greater opportunity to make a difference. I can also be philosophical about the experience of becoming skilled at a job that probably wasn't an ideal match for my abilities. But in the end, I choose to measure my experience by the learning I've done over the last two years. My graduation from college, although I didn't realize it at the time, was just the beginning of my education. Despite the naïveté of not considering more carefully the daily routine of my new job, I did make a wise choice in seeking out a company that would take the time to train me extensively. Over the past couple of years, I've learned a tremendous amount about the world of business, not just from the weeks I spent in training at the corporate headquarters, the mentoring I received from my supervisors, or the seminars and university courses my company enrolled me in, but also simply from the time I've spent in the field learning an industry from the ground up.

I am often called by headhunters asking me to take my skills to another company, something that never would have happened to me if I hadn't acquired the skills from this job. One day I may cash in on the market value of my experience. I may also parlay my young career into a trip to business school. In either case I know that my background stands me in good stead. In any future position, I will draw on both my sales skills and my knowledge of one of America's biggest corporations. It may be most illustrative of all, however, to reveal that as I write this piece, I am awaiting placement in my next assignment. I have finally earned that much-anticipated promotion beyond sales representative. I am now a manager.

Some Advice from David

Gathering Career Advice: A helpful activity for me was thinking about where I wanted to be in my career a few years down the line and then calling up headhunters to find out what kind of experience I'd need to ultimately reach that goal. Coming right out of school, I certainly wasn't going to be a client for these headhunters, but that didn't matter. Such people love to hear themselves talk, and what I learned from them was helpful. You can find them in the Yellow Pages under recruiting or executive recruiting.

Campus Recruiting: Even if you don't have a technical or business degree, it doesn't mean you can't get interviews. Although my English degree didn't carry a lot of weight in other departments, the people in sales seemed to value my skills and background.

Picking Companies: Read everything you can about potential employers—their products, markets, goals, corporate culture—in order to narrow down your list to a manageable number of companies. Just about every company is going to have a sales force, so it makes sense to interview with the ones you find most interesting. A great place to learn about companies is from the company files in your career library or in a business school library. You will discover all sorts of good information—annual reports, newspaper clippings, and brochures.

Finding Out What It's Really Like: Before you take a sales job, ask to spend a day in the field with somebody who is in an equivalent position to the one you're seeking. There's no better way to know exactly what the job is like.

Thinking Ahead: Take a look at what the people above your position are doing. Even if you're not wild about the position they're hiring you for, the job may still be worth it if you think the job you may be promoted into would be fulfilling.

Your Customers: For sales positions, how well you relate to your customers is probably more important than how well you relate with your coworkers. It's very important to ask yourself if you'd want to spend your professional time with the people who will be your customers.

Being Proactive with Your Career: Once you take a job, make sure you get regular appraisals from your managers so you know where you stand. Also, don't be bashful about your successes. Because you're out in the field, your superiors aren't going to know how well you're doing unless you tell them.

A Few Resources to Help You Out

Hoover's Handbook of Emerging Companies: Profiles of America's Most Exciting Growth Enterprises, ed. Patrick J. Spain and James R. Talbot (Austin, Tex. Reference Press, 1994). This reference guide profiles 250 companies, explaining who they are and why they're hot. It also provides lists of specific types of up-and-coming companies—top Hispanic- and black-owned businesses, top technology companies, and so on.

Going to Work: A Unique Guided Tour Through Corporate America, by Lisa Birnbach (New York: Villard Books, 1988). An anecdotal and often humorous perspective on fifty of America's major corporations, written in the same casual style as Birnbach's irreverent college guide.

Built to Last: Successful Habits of Visionary Companies, by James C. Collins and Jerry I. Porras (New York: HarperBusiness/HarperCollins, 1994). A well-written, engaging look at eighteen highly successful and enduring companies. The combination of theory and anecdotal examples makes it both interesting and insightful.

The Best Companies for Women, by Baila Zeitz, Ph.D, and Lorraine Dusky (New York: Simon and Schuster, 1988). Gives information on the fifty best companies in which gender barriers are rare and women are encouraged, if they choose, to combine career with family. It provides company profiles, bottom-line information, benefits, policies, and numbers of women in top managerial positions.

The 100 Best Companies to Work for in America, by Robert Levering and Milton Moskowitz (New York: Plume, 1994). Flip through this thorough resource to learn about everything from Ben and Jerry's ``If it's not fun, why do it?'' attitude to Patagonia's liberal time-off policy to JP Morgan's ludicrous bonus packages.

Pursuing

a Career

in Publishing

Patty Chang Anker

As Patty discovered after college, there is an exciting business side to the making of books. In this essay she sheds some light on what it's like to start out in the publicity department of a large New York publishing house.

It's 9:30 A.M. on a Monday. "You have ten new messages," my voice-mail system informs me. Three requests for review copies. Three producers calling to arrange telephone interviews with authors. Two panicked authors desiring immediate assistance. One producer canceling an interview. My boyfriend calling asking if I'll be working late . . . again. A large stack of newspapers sits in my cubby in the publicity and subsidiary rights department of a New York publishing house. I take a sip of coffee. Another week has begun.

Six months earlier I was sitting in the cluttered office of a friend of a friend, who happened to be an editor in publishing. Intrigued by the idea of working with writers, I had called Paul and asked for an informational interview. Being an editor was the only job that came to mind when I thought of publishing. In between taking messages from a harried-looking assistant, Paul set me straight.

"There's a lot more to publishing than editing," he explained. "If you want to work with unfinished manuscripts and shape them into books, then editorial production or design may be for you. But if you would rather work on getting the finished product into the reader's hands, then there's marketing, advertising, publicity, and subsidiary rights to consider as well."

By the time I stepped out of his office and into Manhattan's rush hour, I had a much better idea of how a publishing company is put together.

THE PUBLISHING PRIMER

As I learned from Paul, an editorial team is responsible for the initial development of a book. Often it starts with the editorial assistants, who lug home piles of manuscripts to read and sift through, pulling out the best to be looked at more closely. They pass these on to editors who acquire the project, negotiate the contract, and help develop the ideas into a book.

As the book starts to take shape, however, there are a slew of other people who also become involved. The marketing department brainstorms ideas for how the book will be positioned in the marketplace and sold. If the book happens to be about apples, for example, they would have several markets to consider: cooks, food columnists, gift book buyers, and orchard owners, to name a few. What is the best way to reach these audiences—promotional giveaways, in-store displays, special discounts to people in apple-growing associations? How much money should go toward advertising? Would the author be good on TV or is a lecture tour more appropriate? How about apple tastings in local bookstores?

Meanwhile, the sales department is busy sending representatives to bookstores across the country. At each stop, these representatives try to sell the publisher's new releases, emphasizing the marketing plans and other commitments the publisher has made to each title. Then there's the team responsible for advertising and promotions. Their artistic canvases are the newspapers, magazines, radio, TV, subway posters, and other creative venues. At the same time, the subsidiary rights department shops the manuscript around, trying to sell book excerpts to magazines, translation rights to foreign publishers, and paperback rights to other publishing houses.

Once the book has been edited, designed, and produced, it's ready to be launched. The publicity department is where that happens. Publicists send out countless books, make hundreds of calls, and create stacks of promotional material, all in hopes of getting the book reviewed and having the author interviewed on radio, TV, and in print. Then to kick it all off, the publicity people also organize bookstore events and publication parties to promote the book's release.

As my background was in media—I majored in communications and had a few public relations internships under my belt by senior year—publicity sounded like the ideal department for me. When an opening for a publicity assistant became available at a publishing house where Paul used to work, I leapt at the chance. After a brief interview in which I promised I could do a hundred things at once and still be smiling, I was hired.

"There's so much work to do that, if you're willing, you could find yourself booking interviews and handling authors very quickly," my new boss promised. Great! With a glamorous career of schmoozing with famous authors in my future, I cheerfully threw myself into the clerical work. How bad could it be, I thought.

Just Me, Myself, and the Cleaning Lady

My first few months as a publicity assistant flew by in a not-so-glamorous blur of ringing telephones, photocopying, faxing, clipping and filing reviews, packing books and packing more books. In order for the world to know about new books (the first step of selling books), someone has to send them to reviewers, television and radio producers, journalists, and influential people. That someone is the publicity assistant. To messenger or not to messenger? Federal Express or 2-Day Air? The guys in the mailroom and copy center became my best friends. During the work week I was deluged with meetings, phone calls, and unexpected emergencies—everything from an earthquake in the city where an author was on tour to a surprise review that sparked interest in an old title. Weekends were often spent reading and writing press releases.

During late evenings, while I was standing in front of the fax machine and filing cabinets, there were times when I wondered why I had been so excited about a career in publishing.

Taking a Step Up

The light at the end of the tunnel was the hope for a promotion. Different publicity departments have different ladders of responsibility, but eventually, every assistant hopes to handle full publicity campaigns, and to have an expense account! Three months into my publishing career, I got my wish. The publicist I was assisting decided to change companies, leaving behind a lot of work to do before another publicist was hired. With all the confidence I could muster, I told my boss I could handle the work in the interim.

I was suddenly immersed in a new world of challenging responsibilities. My book packing role didn't change, but now I was also brainstorming with authors and editors, trying to develop innovative publicity plans that would help our books take off. I was constantly on the lookout for news hooks that would tie the books and authors to current events. Any connection I could find I would work into the two-page press releases that were supposed to summarize the most important, interesting, and newsworthy points of each book. And then I'd be on the phone, calling up the media to offer ways they might incorporate an interview with an author or a mention of one of our books in a story.

When Dan Quayle accused Murphy Brown of being a bad influence on society and the rest of the country was rolling their collective eyes at our vice president's quarrel with a fictional television character, I jumped at the opportunity to get an author, a single mom and an expert on the history of families, to take on Pat Buchanan on CNN. When the World Series came up, it was my job to read everything I could on the economics of baseball to find hooks that would get one of our authors who was an expert on the subject onto sports shows.

Then I got my big break. In the publicist's absence, I found myself responsible for one of our most important new releases—a controversial book by a prominent civil rights leader about the permanence of racism in America. The author's ideas challenged and provoked me, and made me seriously rethink what being Asian-American meant to me. Getting his message out compelled me to take my work with me everywhere, sparking many debates with friends, family members, and coworkers about the racial climate in this country. Each day I was on the phone from the moment the first New York TV and radio producers stepped into their offices until the last producer on the west coast left for the day. In between, I scrambled to schedule lectures, newspaper interviews, and any other publicity events I could drum up.

It was an incredible experience to feel the publicity build around this book that meant so much to me. Hearing friends talk about the book, turning on the television and seeing the author on talk shows, walking into my office and finding a stack of newspaper articles about the book, all made me feel like our efforts were paying off. Then I got the best news of all. "Did you hear? It's on the list!" was the buzz around the office. I was stunned. The book was on the *New York Times* best-seller list! Even now, a few years and a couple of promotions later, I remember that day when, as an assistant, I knew that my work was important, and both professionally and personally, deeply satisfying.

Some Advice from Patty

Looking for a Job: Half the battle of landing a position in publishing is finding out about job openings. Many positions are never advertised, so word of mouth is often your best bet. Mention your interest to anyone and everyone you know. Don't be bashful. You never know who may have some link to the publishing industry—friends, family, classmates, alumni, even professors.

Other Ways to Make Connections: Any big publishing city—New York, Boston, Chicago, San Francisco—will have weekly or monthly social gatherings for people in the publishing industry. These are a great way to meet people on a casual level and learn the latest industry gossip. Also, look for regional book fairs. Being a book fair volunteer can be an ideal way to get into these key publishing schmooze fests for free.

Focusing Your Job Search: If you know what department you would like to work for—production, design, publicity, editorial, sales, subsidiary rights, marketing—then send a letter and résumé directly to the director of that department at each house that interests you. You can find their names in the *Literary Market Place*, which can be found in most libraries. If you are unsure which department you would like to be in, you may want to consider a "floater program" (some houses will hire people to assist in various departments as needed), an internship, or a summer publishing institute (see resources).

Preparing for an Interview: The more you know about the publishing house and current industry news, the better you will be. Scan *Publishers Weekly*, a trade magazine, for news about the publishing house's upcoming titles and projects. Read *The New York Times Book Review* for current books and check out the best-seller lists. Walk through a bookstore to get an idea of which publishers are publishing what.

Network, Network, Network: From your first interview through the rest of your career in publishing, your contacts will provide job leads, inside information on other houses, career advice, as well as professional and emotional support. Once you land a job, keep building your connections by meeting as many people as possible in a wide range of houses. Trade books with other assistants. Tell your professional friends about job openings. Put in the effort to keep your contact list up to date. Success in publishing depends on a combination of who you know, what you know, and being in the right place at the right time. Contacts can help you with all three.

A Few Resources to Help You Out

Literary Market Place (R. R. Bowker, A Reed Reference Publishing Company, New Providence, N.J.). An annually published directory listing book publishers, literary agents, book packagers, book manufacturers, printers, and industry yellow pages.

Publishers Weekly (Cahners Magazines, 249 West 17th Street, New York, N.Y. 10011, [800] 278-2991). This magazine offers current information about the publishing scene—insider reports on auctions, mergers, promotions; marketing and financial analyses; hot books; and author interviews.

Radcliffe Publishing Course (Radcliffe College, 77 Brattle Street, Cambridge, Mass. 02138, [617] 495-8678). A summer professional training program designed for recent college graduates interested in a career in publishing. Applications are accepted from January 1st through April 1st.

The Management Institute Center for Publishing, New York University (48 Cooper Square, Room 108, New York, N.Y. 10023, [212] 998-7219). New York University offers various book publishing courses. Students can enroll on a class-by-class basis. The university also has a publishing certificate program that you can fulfill by completing a certain number of courses.

Howard University Press Book Publishing Institute (Howard University, 1240 Randolph NE, Washington, D.C. 20017, [202] 806-4946). Five weeks of intensive course study focused on book publishing. Courses are conducted by publishing professionals.

Management
Consulting

Jim Migdal

What do you actually do in management consulting? According to Jim, consultants do everything from counting cars coming out of factories to squinting at computer spreadsheets of sock and underwear sales. And while you're at it, you also have a chance to tackle some genuinely interesting business problems.

"Advise the senior management of Fortune 100 companies on business unit strategy...." "Looking for outstanding intellectual ability...." "High impact through our client work...." These are some of the things that caught my eye in the glossy brochures put out by the top consulting firms. I was a political science major who had spent a lot of time pondering the relationship between business and the state, and theorizing about the social implications of market-based economies, but I had never really worked in business. I was looking for an experience that would offer a broader perspective on business operations than what I would get by going into marketing or sales, and management consulting seemed like a good bet.

"If you were the president of a credit card company trying to rethink the economics of your business, how would you go about estimating the value of the average customer's account?" asked the first-round interviewer.

I felt my mouth go dry. OK, forge ahead, I thought, clearing my throat nervously. "Well, on the cost side, I guess I would probably start by seeing how much I spent on advertising to attract a customer. I would also want to look at how much it cost to establish an account in terms of credit checks and processing an application. Then I would start to look at the ongoing costs of processing credit card statements and how long a customer actually remained a customer."

"And if you wanted to lower your cost of customer acquisition, what are some of the issues you would want to think about?" she asked.

"I would try to track how many people signed up based on where they heard about the card, and then . . ."

The questions and answers went back and forth like this for about half an hour as the interviewer pushed me to define the logic of my thinking and to reconsider the assumptions I was making. I knew she was not looking for any right answers but was interested in my approach to the problem. This interview was one of the key things that sold me on management consulting: I liked the idea of working with someone to dissect complex business problems with bottom-line consequences.

What *Is* Management Consulting, Anyway?

"So you work for a management consulting firm. What exactly does *that* mean?" I remember my older sister, the aspiring actress, asking over dinner. As I explained to her, it can mean a lot of different things. A company will hire a consulting firm to deal with problems it doesn't want to handle on its own. For example, if the CEO of a home electronics company wants to get into the personal computer business, he or she will probably hire a consultant to study whether or not that's a good idea. Clients also want consulting firms to bring objectivity and a fresh perspective to their businesses. For example, if a car company took twice as long as the competition to develop a new model, it might bring in a consultant to rethink the way it makes cars as well as to look for ways to do it faster and for less money.

There are an enormous number of firms involved in some aspect of consulting, each with its own particular angle on business. The bigger, "name" firms, like McKinsey, Bain, or Boston Consulting Group, are "generalists" that work on strategy issues for Fortune 100 companies in many different industries. Then there are firms that specialize in a particular industry, like environmental engineering or telecommunications, and niche firms that focus on specific subjects, like human resources or information systems.

BUSINESS WORLD 101

"Net present values, experience curves, ratios analysis"—oh, sure, no problem . . . now. But two years ago, I had never heard of these concepts. Fortunately, the big firms put a lot of effort into training programs to make sure every humanities major can work through a cash-flow analysis. In my first few months on the job, a lot of my time was spent getting the *Reader's Digest* condensed version of business school. On my first day, I found my plain metal desk among a bullpen of six other analysts. On top of it were my business cards, a PC, and a huge three-ring binder of training materials. Every week five other new hires, a trainer, and I would work through a different chapter on cost accounting, presentation skills, financial analysis, competitive analysis, client confidentiality issues, on and on, often until late at night.

The training period ended with an intense two-week program at a resort on Cape Cod. Upon seeing the place, complete with swimming pools, tennis courts, catered meals, and a view of the Atlantic from the living room of the villa, I thought, This is the life. Think again.

The whole time I was there, I walked on the beach only once! Classes started at 8:00 A.M. sharp, and each night my training group and I worked through a business case that applied the concepts we had learned that day. Everybody was a perfectionist, and those evening sessions usually ran until about midnight as we put the final touches on the next morning's presentation. In a demented way, I thrived on it. Management consulting tends to attract people who are tenacious problem solvers. The opportunity to work with these kind of people is part of what makes the training so valuable.

IT's TUESDAY, THIS MUST BE JACKSONVILLE

Firms want you to be creative in gathering information and astute in figuring out what the information means. Ultimately the recommendations they make to clients are based on the integrity of the data you collect. As a first-year, you are at the bottom of the information food chain. You go out and get the data, and then massage out the inconsistencies and exceptions to make it tell the right story. This process can offer some intriguing challenges, but it can also seem monotonous and absurd.

For example, my first project was for a client in the beer can business who wanted a better understanding of the company's expenses. In four months I went from simply knowing how to open a beer can to appreciating the intricacies of different aluminum-stamping techniques.

"The cost of the can itself is actually about 80 percent of the total product cost, so the profit margins are very sensitive to the level of staffing and the type of equipment used in the manufacturing process," a manager explained to a group of us over pizza one Monday evening. "We've gotten as far as we can get in the telephone interviewing, so I want to put some effort into these competitor plant visits."

This was it—my first business trip. Each of us was given an assignment: go out and get the goods on five plants. For the next few hours, we talked about how we could dig up information.

"Through the Clean Air and Water legislation, manufacturing companies have to give their emissions data to the EPA. Most companies include floor plans in their filings...," explained one of the senior analysts.

On Tuesday I was up at 5:30 A.M. to catch a 7:15 flight to Jackson,

Mississippi. It wasn't exactly a glamorous assignment, but I had never been to Mississippi before. The first stop of my thirty-six-hour stay was the EPA office, where I picked up heating and cooling descriptions of the plant along with an electrical wiring diagram. Next stop was the county clerk's office.

"And why is it that you want a copy of the blueprints for the Crown, Cork, and Seal plant, Mr. Migdal, sir?" inquired a heavyset county official in a thick Jackson drawl.

Well, sir, we're spying on them for one of their Yankee competitors, I thought. No, I had better not tell him that. "Just doing a little research project," I mumbled sheepishly. Later that day I sent an E-mail back to the office explaining that I had found the right information on equipment and that all I needed was staffing data.

That night, out on County Highway 187 in my rented white Ford Tempo, I sat in the dark just down the road from the plant entrance, waiting for the shift change. It was 10:45 P.M. and the graveyard shift came on at 11:00. I was ready with my legal pad and mechanical pencil. Here they come—one, two, three . . . I was counting heads to see how many people worked at the plant. At the crack of dawn, I was out on 187 again for the morning shift. A few hours later I flew to Columbia, South Carolina, where I repeated the same drill. Then on to Jacksonville, Florida, and Milwaukee, Wisconsin.

By the time I hit Jacksonville, the ludicrousness of flying around the country gathering wiring diagrams and counting cars coming out of beer can plants was getting to me. But that's part of starting out at the bottom. As a first-year analyst, you think about business strategy part of the time, but most of your effort is spent gathering data and packaging it for someone else to do the serious analysis.

SOCKS AND SPREADSHEETS

In the second year on the job, you have more responsibility. You spend more time doing the analysis while the first-years are out looking for wiring diagrams. In one of my projects, for example, I developed a spreadsheet model to simulate the economics of a cli-

CONSULTANT "004" REPORTING... I HAVE COMPETITOR'S BEER CAN OPERATION IN SIGHT... OVER...

ent's sock business. The client owned the rights to a famous brand name in underwear and wanted to know if it made sense to try farming this name out to socks. Working with a consultant, it was my job to try and figure this out by running numbers. What would be more profitable, selling brand-name Gold Toe socks or making private label socks for other companies? Would the company be better off selling at premium department stores like Macy's or mass-market chains like Wal-Mart?

These were the kinds of issues I was trying to tackle with my models. By the end of the project, I had spent about three months in front of a souped-up PC playing out different scenarios of what the client might do. By the last couple of weeks, I walked, talked, and ate socks. Working twelve-hour days, seven days a week, I felt that I was really starting to understand the business. The payoff came with a trip to Chicago when we rolled out the dog and pony show for the client's CEO. He and his team picked through every assumption in the model and I sat by quietly as my boss sweated through their questions. Based on our recommendations, they changed their licensing agreements with several different companies and ended up repositioning their products completely. I couldn't believe that this billion-dollar company would actually change its whole operation based on the tinkering I had done with a few spreadsheets!

THE BIG PICTURE

At times, consulting seemed like a charade: millions of dollars spent to gather blueprints and a lot of white shirts talking about making beer cans as if they were negotiating at Yalta. But I found that there really is an element of excitement to consulting. People bring an intellectual intensity to their work that's hard to find in the business world. Yes, at times I may take a step back and laugh at it, but debating things like the virtues of selling private label socks over branded socks can be an intense and satisfying experience. It's not the socks, or beer cans, or whatever other product you're dealing with, it's the process of working with a dynamic group of people trying to come up with new ways to answer open-ended questions. As an analyst, much of what you do falls on the less glamorous side of the consulting process—counting workers and squinting at microscopic spreadsheets—but you're still part of a challenging, problem-solving effort. For me, it was just the right angle to look at the sometime absurd, sometime fascinating world of business.

Some Advice from Jim

Getting an Interview: Big firms see a lot of résumés and bland cover letters, so being persistent will give you a better shot at getting an interview. Call to be sure the right person is looking at your résumé and ask if you can talk with someone about your qualifications. The firm that eventually hired me lost my résumé three times before I actually had an interview.

Handling Rejection Letters: If you get a rejection letter and really want an interview, send a follow-up letter or pick up the phone to make your case again. The first screen by the personnel office can be somewhat arbitrary, and you want to do everything you can to avoid being lost in the shuffle.

Talking the Talk: Consulting has its own peculiar culture and mindset. To understand it, it helps to be steeped in the lingo. Before you interview, take a look at Michael Porter's books on competitive strategy and read through an issue or two of *Harvard Business Review*. This will give you an idea of how consulting types think. It may also help you decide if consulting is for you, depending on whether you find yourself chomping at the bit or nodding off after the first few pages.

Walking the Walk: When you first start out as an analyst, you'll get a few "soft" assignments designed to test you out before they let you do anything of substance. Be extremely thorough—make sure the numbers add up and the spelling is correct—so they'll be willing to trust you with more responsibility down the road. Otherwise you'll end up with a steady diet of drudgery because you're weak on "due diligence."

Hitting the Ground Running: Like an essay in college, consulting projects can always be improved. When you finish an assignment and are about to show your work to your boss, think about the logical next steps. If you think hard about what you might do to improve your analysis and about questions that your work raises for the rest of the project, your boss will be likely to see that you are pushing to take things to the next level.

A Few Resources to Help You Out

Competitive Strategy: Techniques for Analyzing Industries and Competitors, by Michael E. Porter (New York: Free Press/Macmillan, 1980). You'll find this on nearly every consultant's bookshelf. It contains the theories and ideas behind management consulting and is invaluable for getting up to speed for interviews.

Harvard Business Review. A monthly periodical that contains the latest theory, validated through real-life examples from the business world. It's a little pricey, so you might want to try the library before you hit the newsstand.

Harvard Business School Career Guide—Management Consulting, ed. Sue C. Marsh (Boston: Harvard Business School Press, 1994). Profiles the top consulting firms. Although this guide is written primarily for business school graduates, it's still the best resource for undergraduates wanting to get the specifics on prospective firms. It's not sold in bookstores, but you may find it at your college career center.

The Directory of Management Consultants (Fitzwilliam, N.H.: Kennedy Publications, 1995). A comprehensive directory from the publishers of *Consultant News* that profiles over thirteen hundred firms, indexed by services offered, industry, and geography. Check your career center or business school library for this publication.

Rebels with a Cause

There's no question that college offers a rare forum for lively discussions about how the world might be improved. Coffee shops, library lobbies, class papers, and campus rallies all provide an opportunity to voice thoughts and opinions about issues such as racism, where our public education system has gone astray, how our natural environment is being degraded, and why developing nations are considered disadvantaged. This discourse can be insightful and inspiring, but at a certain point, discussion and debate alone can start to get old. Talk is talk, but what can you actually do to turn academic banter into real-world action?

Perhaps it was this question that inspired Wendy Kopp as she searched for a senior thesis topic back in 1989. During her years of academic discourse, two important ideas had become unified in her mind—first, that our underfunded and overbureaucratized public school system needed more teachers, and second, that many of her soon-to-be graduated colleagues would relish the opportunity to give something back to the public school system, especially if there was a practical way to become involved. In her thesis, Wendy proposed a solution that addressed both of these issues—a program, funded largely by corporate America, that would recruit and train eager graduates to spend their first two years after college teaching in disadvantaged public school districts. After graduation, Wendy took her idea and turned it into a reality. Now in its sixth successful year, Teach For America has provided inner-city and rural school districts with over three thousand committed teachers and has offered an equal number of college graduates the opportunity to give something back to their communities.

Like many college students before her, Wendy had ideas about what could be done to improve the world, but what's inspiring about her story is that she developed a powerful bridge between those abstract theories and concrete action. Making that link is what this section of the book is about.

If there are issues you feel strongly about, or you simply want to offer help where it's needed most, why not take advantage of the time you have after graduation to find your own link to action? Six months out of college you could be six thousand miles from home providing basic health education in an African village; or you could be Washington, D.C., working to promote change on a policy level; or you could combine hands-on service with policy work by writing grants for a community organization you believe in; or you could even spend your days working with inner-city students as a part of Wendy's Teach For America program.

These are not always easy paths to take—trying to address intractable problems inevitably involves frustrations and sometimes even failure. But in spite of these challenges, few who opt for this kind of postcollege experience would choose to be elsewhere.

As you will see in the essays that follow, making a personal commitment to an issue or organization you believe in can be one of the most fulfilling solutions to that quandary of what to do after graduation.

Teach For America

Andy McKenzie

Teach For America is a unique opportunity for recent graduates to give something back to the community by teaching for two years in an inner-city or rural public school. In this essay, Andy uses his own teaching tales to highlight some of the sources of frustration and fulfillment of this intense experience.

The Nile River flooded right on schedule that Tuesday afternoon in room 5. Despite the fact that it was running in a Los Angeles elementary school thousands of miles from its Egyptian homeland, the Nile managed to wind its way through my classroom and over-flow its banks to an approving chorus of hoots and hollers from twenty-nine fifth and sixth graders.

We had spent the better part of the morning constructing a clay river valley that snaked across a giant baker's cake pan filled with sandy dirt. Before the flooding began, we had all gathered around our handiwork in hushed expectation: José held a bucket full of water over one end of the pan. Three and a half feet away, Omar held an empty bucket under the pan's other end, which jutted several inches off the edge of the table.

"OK," I began, "before we start, who remembers what this bump in the riverbed is called? Rosa?"

"It's a cataract. It's like a little waterfall," she said.

"Right. How many big cataracts does the real Nile have, Manuel?"

"Five?"

"Stupid," Andrea interjected. "It's got six, Mr. McKenzie."

"That's right, but I think we can be a little more polite about it. Um, Yvonne, where do you want your farm?"

"Right here by the, um, the, um, triangle part."

"That's too easy," José said. "It always floods by the delta. Take a chance."

"OK, right here," she said, pushing a twig into the dirt five inches off the left bank of the river. Five other students claimed farmland in the cake pan and prayed for a flood over their property.

I then gave José the green light and he began to pour steadily. Water ran over the cataract, down through the twisting river valley, out through the delta region, and into Omar's bucket. As José increased the water, the brimming river overflowed, turning most parts of the pan into mud. Yvonne, Eneida, Rene, Brenda, and Cesar would reap large harvests as ancient Egyptian farmers. Only Cynthia's farmland remained dry. She would have to trade for food that year.

Thirty minutes later, as we wrapped up our discussion of the day's experiment, Rene raised his hand rather shakily. I called on him.

"Omar should have been standing over there," he said, pointing. "We should have turned the table."

"Why?" I asked, genuinely intrigued.

"Because over there is north, and, you know, the Nile flows north, doesn't it?"

"I'm glad you remembered," I said, completely stunned. "You're absolutely right, it does flow northward."

These delicious moments—however scattered, scarce, and dearly earned—when students are thinking, working together, enjoying their learning, and even teaching their teacher, are what can make Teach For America such a fulfilling way to spend your first two years out of college.

It would be misleading to suggest that Teach For America is only about such magic moments, for in truth it has more than its fair share of frustrating and difficult times. There are plenty of days when you'll present a lesson you think is brilliant, only to see it sail right over the heads of your confused class. Or perhaps you don't even get the chance to complete the lesson, because much of your energy is expended simply trying to maintain control over a classroom full of mutinous children. Then there are the daily demands of resolving minor scuffles and volleys of name-calling, and the odd occasion when you walk to the principal's office with the collar of a student in one hand and the pocketknife he brought to class in the other. Or you're sitting in a staff meeting, learning that the already meager allotment of photocopies you're granted each week for class assignments and handouts has been cut in half. And, finally, there are all of those late-night sessions when your college classmates who took nine-to-five jobs are fast asleep and you're still sitting at your desk trying to come up with tomorrow's lesson plan.

But somehow, when a lesson works, when a series of lessons culminates in a meaningful class project, or when one child solves a previously confounding problem, then those frustrations seem unimportant.

Ultimately, Teach For America is about children, and every day that you rise to the challenge of teaching them, they stand a better chance of succeeding. It is also a way to give something back for the education you've received . . . and get an enormous amount in return.

WHO JOINS TEACH FOR AMERICA?

The "typical" Teach For America teacher doesn't exist. If you polled program participants today, you'd find recent graduates who majored in everything from computer science, biochemistry, and

philosophy to art history, semiotics, and, yes, even education. Ask them about future plans and you'll get stories about medical school, business jobs, staying in teaching, becoming involved in education policy, and a multitude of other endeavors. This diversity is partly a result of the unique lure of Teach For America: so many people coming out of college have some desire to teach but are rebuffed by the time and financial commitment that are traditionally required to be certified. By committing two years to TFA, you're able to act on that desire—being put almost immediately into the class-room—and still move on to other career goals afterward.

Teach For America can also provide some relief from career angst. For me, it was a chance to get some distance and perspective before I took my next big step in life. As a senior, I was convinced that life after college meant graduate school studying Russian litera-ture (a prolonged stay in the intellectual arena that was my comfort zone). Somewhere along the way, I began to lose my passion and drive for digesting novels and writing esoteric commentaries. As my academic focus clouded, I began to reevaluate. I realized that I was burned out on the whole college gig and needed an adventure—something, ideally, that would be useful to me and to others as well. With that thought in mind, I decided to shelve my graduate studies and join Teach For America.

The Summer Institute

The two-year Teach For America term begins at the TFA summer training institute in Los Angeles. Together with several hundred other corps members—hailing from different universities, home-towns, ethnic and cultural backgrounds, and philosophical and political camps—I went through an eight-week crash course, boot camp–like blitz in the fundamentals of teaching. Part lectures, discussions, and workshops, part student teaching experience in the classroom, it's an opportunity to get your feet wet while there's still someone at the edge of the pool to hold your hand. Working with a mentor teacher, you'll observe lessons, write lesson plans, tutor individual students, teach small groups of students, and eventually teach a whole class the entire school day for two weeks. This practice run is an invaluable opportunity to collect useful teaching strategies and techniques, try them out, and, most important, learn from your mistakes.

My unspectacular debut as a student teacher was a geography lesson that, ironically, included the Nile. Unlike the river flooding I orchestrated a year and a half later, it was far from successful. Attempting to teach my class how to read the key of a climate map of Africa, I used the Nile as a point of reference, as if it were as familiar to the students as the bus stop on the corner. Not surprisingly, no one knew what or where it was, and I didn't take any time to stop and explain. Why? I was miming what I had known so intimately: the college professor's meandering style of lecture that depends on huge stores of background knowledge for comprehension—hardly something appropriate for fifth and sixth graders. This is the kind of mistake any fledgling teacher will make, and having an experienced teacher there to help point it out and suggest alternatives is one of the things that makes the summer institute such a valuable experience.

All too soon, however, the summer ends and, in a blur, the corps members part ways—you move to a new city or town, you try to locate your assigned school on a map, you meet your new principal, you script your first week of teaching, you unlock your classroom door, you flip on the lights, you assemble your props, you rehearse your lines, you wonder what you've gotten yourself into, and then, with the crash of the eight o'clock bell, you realize that, ready or not, it's show time.

THE FIRST YEAR

For most teachers, the first year of Teach For America is a uniquely challenging experience, lightly seasoned with triumphs and break-throughs. Being entrusted with the education and guidance of thirty youngsters is a staggering responsibility, and there's a lot that takes getting used to.

The adjustments start the moment you set foot in your new school. Teach For America places its teachers in parts of the country where they're needed most, which means you'll end up teaching either in a small rural town or smack in the middle of a large city.

Being placed in Los Angeles, I was faced with the initial challenge of attuning myself to what my students faced outside the classroom. Encountering graffiti, gangs, and violence was all too common for my seasoned ten- and eleven-year-olds. I was speechless the first time one of my girls said, "Oh, I didn't finish my homework because they shot someone near my apartment last night and the sirens scared me, so I just went to sleep." Knowing that's what your kids may find when they leave your class can be deflating. But at the same time, it can help motivate you to make those precious hours together that much more meaningful and positive.

Your next rapid reality check comes in time management. Any visions a new TFA member may have had when he or she signed up of spending afternoons after class lounging around the pool are recognized within the first week for what they are—purely delusional thoughts. While my time card said 7:30 A.M. to 2:30 P.M., I quickly found out that 6:00 A.M. to 6:00 P.M. barely covered the entire job. Those long hours spent outside the classroom for planning, correcting papers, staying on top of official paperwork, and brainstorming demand a tight schedule.

I never joined the Boy Scouts as a kid, but I heartily endorsed their motto after my first year of teaching. My roommate, another TFA teacher, was told by his principal with annoying frequency, "If you fail to plan, you plan to fail," and it was true. As a first-year teacher, much of your energy is devoted to preparation. You plan, you plan some more, and then you keep planning. But inevitably you come up short, and then it's time to improvise. Nothing approaches that sinking feeling you experience during the first month when lessons and activities that you planned for sixty or ninety minutes end neatly after thirty or forty:

"So, what are we doing next, Mr. McKenzie?"

"We're going to, um . . . um, we're going to sing! Yup, we're going to sing 'When the Saints Go Marching In.' In rounds. Who knows what a round is? Well, first we'll have to write the lyrics. Paper monitors, please pass out paper. . . ."

As the year moves forward, however, you find yourself becoming more and more adept at putting together lessons and keeping your class engaged. You develop a stronger relationship with your kids, you realize which projects, activities, and strategies work and which don't, and you finally get used to being called by your last name. Who knows exactly where it happens, but somewhere between the moment you enter the summer institute and the day you let your kids go the following summer, a transformation occurs: you become a teacher.

THE SECOND YEAR AND BEYOND

In your second year you'll experience many of the same ups and downs that you weathered during the first year, but there's a difference—now you have the benefit of experience. All of your improvisational skills and prior planning are a tremendous asset, giving you the chance to both perfect what you've already done and continue to chart new teaching territory.

What happens at the end of that second year is up to you. As for me, I chose to stay on at my school for one more year, and now, in three weeks I'm off to graduate school. Although my time as an elementary school teacher in Los Angeles is over, the experience will continue to shape who I am and what I do, for as a Teach For America member, I have learned far more than I have taught. The children I've spent my days with have selflessly taught me a great deal about themselves and about myself. Together we have experienced frustration and success, felt sadness and elation, acted plain silly, and tried to reach farther than we thought we ever could.

I walk away from my Teach For America experience knowing that in spite of the adversity they face, students in the inner city have the courage and tenacity to set and pursue daring goals. As a teacher, you can provide them with the support and tools to help nourish and encourage their dreams. In my mind, the real heroes are the people who have taught in these schools, showing passion and devotion day in and day out for years. For anyone leaving college, having the opportunity to work alongside these teachers for a couple of years can be a tremendous experience. It was for me.

Some Advice from Andy

Gathering Ideas: Every good teacher is an accomplished thief. You should take good teaching ideas from every possible source and use them. Copy successful techniques from other teachers. Repeat interesting projects you see other classes working on. Ask questions of your peers. Distill everything you learn and use your ideas and creativity to make it your own.

Unlearning: Do not assume anything. Be as explicit as possible when you introduce new ideas. You may need to imaginatively "unlearn" what you already know about something to understand what it may be like to learn it anew. As I had to keep reminding myself, many things that are second nature to you may be absolutely foreign ideas to your students.

Classroom Management: Perhaps the hardest task you'll face early on is establishing and maintaining control of your class. I've found that if I make my rules very clear from day one and I stick to them, exercising consistency and fairness at every possible turn, I'll gain the trust of my students and they will understand what I expect of them. Remember, you are a role model. Even your firmest reactions to problems should be dealt out with respect.

Teaching Everything: Elementary school teachers are called on to teach all subjects to their students. Whether or not you majored in science, you'll teach it. A typical day may include lessons on Egyptian tombs, long division, photosynthesis, writing, mixing paint colors, and techniques in spiking a volleyball. To stay ahead, learn as much as you can from the resources at your school—books, teachers, students.

A Few Resources to Help You Out

Teach For America (P.O. Box 5114, New York, N.Y. 10185, [800] 832-1239). TFA members go through a summer training program and then spend two years teaching at a public school in an inner-city or rural area. The program requires a 2.5 GPA or higher. Before you start teaching, you must have completed your bachelor's degree. Call to request an application.

Inner-City Teaching Corps (2648 West Pershing Road, Chicago, Ill. 60632, [312] 579-0150). This program is similar to TFA but works on a smaller scale. ICTC recruits recent college graduates to teach in the inner city of Chicago. Unlike in TFA, ICTC teachers also live together in modest community housing. ICTC offers a summer training institute followed by two years of teaching. Call to request an application.

National Association of Independent Schools (75 Federal Street, Boston, Mass. 02110, [617] 451-2444). Private schools are another option for college graduates interested in teaching who may not have the necessary credentials. Call for a listing of placement agencies and other useful information about finding a position at an independent school.

36 Children, by Herbert Kohl (New York: Plume Publishing/Penguin Books, 1967). A true account of an innovative and open-minded young teacher's year with a Harlem sixth-grade class.

Stand and Deliver. A powerful movie based on the true story of an inspirational math teacher in inner-city Los Angeles. Any good video store should have it.

Savage Inequalities: Children in America's Schools, by Jonathan Kozol (New York: Crown, 1991). A chilling look at the adversity children and teachers face in low-income neighborhoods.

Joining the
Peace Corps

Brigid Andrew

According to its motto, the Peace Corps is "the toughest job you'll ever love." In this essay, Brigid, who is spending her first two years out of college in Mali, Africa, gives an honest and introspective look at the life of a Peace Corps volunteer.

There is a Fulani proverb that says, "Juude didi lootindira so laaba," or "Two hands must wash each other to be clean." To the herders of the Niger River delta just south of the Sahara Desert, it evokes the notions of reciprocity, interdependence, and mutual assistance. You can put one hand in some water, but the results will always be better if there is a joint effort. I first heard the proverb shortly after I arrived in West Africa as a Peace Corps trainee, and the people of Mali have spent the past year and a half teaching me what it means as we share a simple and often difficult life. I trade preventative health education for the wisdom of an ancient culture and the experience of a lifetime. I try to play the role of my proverbial hand well, but while my original motives may have been altruistic, there is no doubt that I have come out ahead in this exchange.

Living as a Peace Corps volunteer has provided me with some of the most rewarding and unforgettable moments of my life. But be assured, I've earned them by paying heavy dues in frustration, loneliness, and sometimes painful disillusionment. I applied to the Peace Corps halfway through my senior year of college, wanting to exploit my years of academic learning for the benefit of people in need while widening my knowledge of the world and myself. Maybe I'd even figure out what direction my life should take in the process. As a history major, I didn't have enough conviction about my future to make any moves toward a particular career, but I was ready to get out of the classroom and test myself with problems more immediate and real than why Rome fell.

PATIENCE AND FLEXIBILITY

When I applied I had no idea where or when I'd be going abroad and only a vague idea of what I'd be doing. The first six months involved a lot of paperwork, recommendations, medical exams, interviews, and a great deal of waiting. Graduation came and I remember responding to the typical inquires about my next move: "I could be going to Timbuktu for all I know." Ironically, a year later I had just finished the three-month intensive language and technical training and been posted only a hundred miles from that city, which only meant the end of the earth to me in college. The application process is long and full of anxiety because you put your life on hold waiting to qualify and to be cleared. I didn't know it at the time, but I was already being taught the first rule of Peace Corps service: patience.

And then you're on a plane with your job assignment in hand: Mali, health/nutrition education agent. Perhaps you were prepared to be teaching English in Poland or gardening in Bolivia. Because programs, countries, and assignments vary so much (in Mali, for example, there are agents in water/sanitation, forestry, small enterprise development, basic education, gardening, and health), you soon learn that the second most essential quality of a Peace Corps volunteer is flexibility and the willingness to accept, adapt, and work with what you get.

THE HARDSHIPS

On the top of your welcome package, the familiar words haunt you: "The toughest job you'll ever love." A year into my service, I can say the ad campaign writers are right in that it is tough. The Peace Corps is not for everyone. Depending on your placement, you have to adapt and endure a variety of adversities including: no running water, no electricity, eating rice or millet at every meal for two years, no beer, 120-degree temperatures, gastrointestinal parasites, malarial mosquitoes, and scorpions.

One of the hardest things to give up is your privacy and personal space. In general, the Peace Corps is not for someone who likes to keep a low profile. It is exhausting to be a perpetual source of fascination and incessant attention. I have been in Mali for eighteen months now, but the sight of me pulling water from my well still draws an audience of ten or more. But though you are constantly surrounded by people, the Peace Corps can be very lonely and alienating. You learn how much family and friends and familiar culture mean to you as you cope with the isolation and discomforts inherent in being out of your element. Support from home in spirit, letters, and care packages is essential. Think twice about disappearing for two years if things are unstable at home and significant others aren't behind you on this.

Despite the "24/7" (meaning: twenty-four hours a day and seven days a week) aspect of operating as an outsider in a foreign world, the Peace Corps public relations department misleadingly uses the word *job*. It depends on the specific assignment you are given, but being a volunteer rarely feels like a job in any traditional sense of the word. The goals and means are vague and you often find yourself ill prepared to confront the problems you see: 50 percent child mortality, an encroaching desert, rampant sickness, less than 10 percent literacy. There is plenty of work to be done, but as a volunteer, your resources and training are limited and you often have little direction or supervision from the office or your local collaborators. In Mali at least, most volunteers complain that they don't feel useful enough. They spend too much time sitting around idle or just hanging out in their village. Your conscience is your boss, and if you are not self-motivated, you probably won't make it for long.

To be sure, we take advantage of the lack of structure in our work as well. When I'm at the end of my rope, I don't have to wait until five to motorcycle the fifty miles to the regional capital, where I usually find some other volunteers. There we can enjoy a beer and watch the sun set over the Niger as we vent our frustrations and disappointments.

THE REWARDS

Compared to having a job in the States, volunteers may not feel like they're working much, unless they consider the cultural integration process work—learning and adopting the languages, customs, and beliefs of a foreign culture. Actually, being an active participant in an alien environment is perhaps the most satisfying aspect of being a volunteer. When I first arrived in my village, my "host/father/mentor" presented himself to me: "You will eat at my house and I will teach you Fulani. Your name will be Roki Dja." I couldn't imagine then how much this new identity would become a part of me and how completely I would become a part of this community. At the time, it was hard to conceive that I would prefer to eat with my hand out of a communal bowl than off my own individual plate, that I would dye my feet and hand with henna for Ramadan, bathe in the river with my friends at sundown, milk cows and sheep and converse about the most personal and political things in Fulani with people I can honestly consider friends. The relative comfort I have achieved here and the appreciation the people have for my efforts help compensate for the absence of satisfaction on the development or professional front.

I always have to remind myself that development time is painfully slow and that few volunteers ever see the results of their efforts. You rarely have concrete projects whose success you can see or evaluate. It is definitely only a drop in the bucket. In one-on-one interactions, however, there are some fantastic moments when you recognize how important that drop in the bucket can be. In my first three months of service, I helped save a baby from dying of dehydration due to chronic diarrhea. It took no more than some sugar-salt water, nutritious porridges, vigilant encouragement, and compassion. In assisting with births, helping local midwives improve their hygiene and knowledge, you affect the lives of women you know and the children they have. I could work as a nurse in the States for ten years and still not make that kind of contribution, and I'd need a lot more training to do it. The opportunity to have that much of an impact on people has given me a taste of responsibility and usefulness that I didn't know in college.

LEARNING FROM ADVERSITY

To be honest, however, such moments are rare. I also watched my adoptive family's one-year-old baby die from cerebral malaria in less than twelve hours as I stood by helpless, too far from decent medical facilities to do anything. All around me countless others suffer the effects of drought, dwindling natural resources, malnutrition, AIDS, poverty, and disempowerment. Too often my job seems irrelevant to their lives. People want gifts of money and medicine (and often they are accustomed to getting them from "first worlders," who look like Peace Corps volunteers but have a lot more resources). Education is not an identified priority and they can be rather fatalistic about the inevitability of hardship and death. How can I expect people who don't have enough to eat to come to prenatal-counseling sessions? I don't know how many nutrition lessons I have held for an audience of two or three silent women. Who knows what they understand and if they ever change their behaviors because of it? It can be pretty depressing and aggravating not to have the solutions to these problems, to live in a perpetual state of crisis and insecurity. Those are the days when I'm glad I did the work of cultural integration and I can go to friends. Here I am learning to deal with hardship, helplessness, and despair from the pros—people who have managed gracefully, with so little, for centuries.

These are skills I will keep with me. I hope that my efforts to share the daily struggles to get by are felt by those around me, that my technical or analytical skills and my moral support help those who face these conditions for a lifetime. Any volunteer will tell you that what you give is never enough compared to what you receive. At the end of two years, I don't expect the proverbial pair of hands to be noticeably cleaner, but I have discovered the absolute value and motivating force of reciprocity. Regardless of the results, the action of joint participation, give and take, justifies itself. I have taught some about the necessity of change and individual opportunity and learned much about the value of cohesive community, respect for tradition, and the importance of living simply. I like to think that both my adoptive and home cultures will be enriched by the exchange. I know myself better and have more specific ideas about what I want to do with my life than I did sitting in that history seminar two years ago. Whatever work I choose to do will be in some sense development work, which is, at its essence, about empowering people and problem solving. The Peace Corps taught me some of the skills I need to make problems common and solvable. It also gave me the chance to discover how rich and varied the paybacks for that kind of work can be. Like most volunteers, I await my return, newly hardened but also inspired, to see the real benefits of this experience.

Some Advice from Brigid

Applying: Apply early—a year before you'll be available and want to leave. Given the bureaucracy you're dealing with, it's important to be organized and stay on top of all the paperwork. If you do not, you could very easily be held up for something minor, waiting six months or more. By the same token, get your interview early. It's the only way to find out whether there's a program you qualify for or how to become qualified.

Where You Go: It really helps to be flexible about where you're willing to volunteer. If you are open to a range of regions and countries, there's a much better chance that you will be selected and the placement process will be quicker.

Learning the Ropes: The best way to prepare for your assignment is to talk to former Peace Corps volunteers. Once you have been assigned to your post, talk to returning volunteers from that country or technical program. Ask them specifics: What kind of work should I expect? What are the living conditions? What should I bring?

Being Honest with Yourself: In this essay I've done my best to give an honest representation of my experience. At times being a Peace Corps volunteer can be rewarding, but it is also filled with frustration, disappointment, and hardship. I still feel I made the right decision to join, and I don't want to discourage anyone from thinking about it, but if you are considering this option, I want to urge you to keep asking yourself whether you really want to do it—from the moment you consider applying to the day you finish your training. It is a commitment. You should be sure that you want to do it, that you can maintain your motivation and put up with the frustration even if it doesn't turn out to be what you expected or hoped for.

A Few Resources to Help You Out

Peace Corps (806 Connecticut Avenue NW, Washington, D.C. 20526, [800] 424-8580). This U.S. government agency sends American volunteers to work in developing countries. You commit to three months of intensive language and cultural training followed by two years of service. In exchange for your efforts, the Peace Corps will pay for all major expenses. You also receive a readjustment allowance at the end of your term—currently $200 per month of service and training. Call or write for more information.

Alternatives to the Peace Corps: A Directory of Third World and U.S. Volunteer Opportunities, by Annette Olson (Oakland, Calif.: Institute for Food and Development Policy, 1994). Offers extensive listings of international and U.S. voluntary service organizations, study tours, and alternative travel groups.

Volunteer! The Comprehensive Guide to Voluntary Service in the U.S. and Abroad, ed. Max Terry (New York: Council on International Educational Exchange and Commission on Voluntary Service and Action, 1995). A guide to hundreds of short-, medium-, and long-term opportunities in every corner of the world. If you can't find it at your bookstore or career library, contact the Council on International Educational Exchange (205 East Forty-second Street, New York, N.Y. 10017, [212] 661-1414).

Taking Off: Extraordinary Ways to Spend Your First Year Out of College, by Lauren Tarshis (New York: Simon and Schuster, 1989). An inspirational book written by a recent graduate who wanted to find fulfilling alternatives to traditional postcollege avenues. It includes valuable information on domestic and international volunteer opportunities as well as some tantalizing outdoor jobs.

VISTA for
a Year

Daniel Baer

Join AmeriCorps VISTA and you could be providing support at a women's shelter, writing grants to build low-income housing, helping redesign a literacy education program, or working at an inner-city after-school program. In exchange for a one-year commitment, VISTA volunteers receive a stipend and a heavy dose of the realities of the nonprofit world. And now, thanks to AmeriCorps, volunteers also receive $4,725 toward future graduate education. Here are Daniel's reflections on what he experienced when he chose to work for an AIDS foundation in Texas.

Nothing epitomizes the bittersweet character of my year in San Antonio better than the ecstasy and agony of Tex-Mex food. While I was becoming a connoisseur of chalupas, tamales, and barbecued turkey legs, I was eating lunch every day with people who found they were unable to keep down the comino-and-cilantro-spiced dishes they'd been raised on.

The San Antonio AIDS Foundation's dining room, with its beige-and-green-checked linoleum floor, its giant tank of red Kool-Aid, and its endless supply of bent forks, is where I usually lingered, absorbing whatever information the grapevine would pass on to me about this HIV community. Of course, the dining room was not just a place to hang out, it was also a place to eat. The people across the table from me picked at their lunches for more than an hour without making a dent in them. Then there were some people who already knew that no matter how badly their wasting bodies needed calories and nutrients, a bowl of soup was all they could manage.

Because the San Antonio AIDS Foundation had never had the funding to hire a dietitian, the search for foods that would stay down—the search for continuing health—was often a blind one for the clients who ate their meals there. When I saw a notice about federal funding for community nutrition programs, I thought, Aha, this is the kind of thing I'm here to help them obtain.

Little by little I tried to piece together a proposal for funding a nutrition program. When I started working on the nutrition grant, Martin Hernandez, one of the foundation clients I became closest to, was still telling me stories about his favorite enchiladas. Somewhere in the middle of the process, Martin actually taught me to make enchiladas. By the time I was putting the finishing touches on the proposal, Martin was wasting away, uninterested in eating anything besides grapes.

While I was learning a lot about nutrition and even more about living with AIDS, I was also learning that development work—fund-raising, grant writing, and public relations—has become the last hope of a nonprofit sector besieged during the eighties and nineties, as government funding has disappeared and community-based organizations have stepped up their efforts to compete for private dollars. For agencies that don't have the money to hire a development staff, VISTA volunteers seem to be an ideal solution, although VISTAs in development positions certainly defy the popular sixties and seventies image of VISTA volunteers as down-in-the-trenches community organizers.

The whole idea of VISTA has always been to bring skilled people into impoverished communities and create programs that last beyond the one year of VISTA service. In the sixties and seventies, that usually meant that VISTA volunteers would recruit and train members of impoverished communities to run some kind of project that would then keep going long after the volunteers have disappeared. In the eighties and nineties, social service agencies are so strapped for funds that raising money has taken precedence over community organizing. Since money—like a community project—is a lasting legacy, development work conveniently fits right into the VISTA tradition.

JUST DO IT?

Why would a college graduate want to do office work such as writing grant proposals, planning benefit events, or putting out press releases, in some out-of-the-way locale for $600 a month?

If you are looking for something more than material rewards and don't mind spending a good chunk of time feeling frustrated, then VISTA might be for you. If you think it sounds crazy to even think about spending a good chunk of time feeling frustrated, then you might as well cross VISTA off your list of options. VISTA is certainly not for everybody. But let me explain why I was happy enough with my VISTA experience to extend my term of service even after my year commitment was completed.

VISTA is a cultural adventure I didn't want to leave. You don't have to leave the United States to find the sort of total unfamiliarity that draws people to India or Thailand or Peru. There's something to be said for discovering another part of this country and coming to love it the way you might come to love another part of the world. For me, becoming a part of the San Antonio HIV community didn't just mean going to see *La Cage aux Folles* with a bunch of drag queens. It meant actually donning women's lingerie and parading up and down a runway of six picnic tables pushed together. Becoming part of the community also meant learning George Strait songs, buying my first pair of cowboy boots, and going to see my friends compete in barrel-racing and pole-bending competitions at horse shows south of town.

VISTA provides an entrée into communities that few recent college graduates would otherwise come to know from the inside. In San Antonio there were VISTAs providing job training for deaf people (sign language became a major means of communication at all of their parties). Others were working at literacy programs; organizing public-housing residents seeking ownership of their homes; helping to set up a legal aid program for people with AIDS; and ironing out the kinks in a new transitional-living program for the homeless.

THE PEOPLE

Even though my official job description called for me to spend my time developing a grant-writing program at the AIDS Foundation, I spent a good amount of time befriending its clients. My supervisors at the foundation generally shared this commitment. As part of VISTA, part of my role was to think about how my activities fit into the foundation's larger picture. VISTA preservice orientation makes clear that the program is about thinking of the best ways to achieve broad goals and then doing what is necessary to achieve them.

I saw it as part of my express purpose to eat lunch with the clients, to get to know them and to learn to care about them as individuals. I did so in part to understand their needs so that I could prepare a grant proposal that would best serve them. These lunches allowed me to spend time with Lee Hicks, in whose video I played the role of the fundamentalist preacher; Dick McCord, who cut my hair in the foundation's barber shop; and Martin, whose stories of traveling across the country in boxcars I never tired of hearing, even though his dementia left him unable to remember how many times he'd already told me the same story. All of these people and dozens more, most of whom have died now, have shaped my outlook on life. Their lives have molded me into a person I never would have become had I spent my postcollege years working among other privileged college graduates, for whom the future means everything.

The Work

My willingness to go on at such length about the personal rewards of my VISTA experience might make you suspicious about the rewards of the work itself. I learned that in the world of nonprofit community organizations—and even more so in the world of AIDS service organizations—there is endless political wrangling over which groups are going to get the inadequate supply of funds available. Antagonism between various AIDS service agencies in San Antonio was not even politely covered up. It was open warfare between the AIDS Foundation, BEAT-AIDS (an African-American agency), and HACER (a Latino agency). It was ugly. And here I was, the new grant-writing VISTA, dropped down in the middle of the battlefield.

But like many VISTA volunteers seem to do, I tried hard to find a niche for myself where I could do some good without getting in anybody else's way. I researched government funding opportunities and private foundations that might give grants to an AIDS service organization, then talked to the AIDS Foundation's staff and clients about what sort of needs they could see grants addressing and started putting grant proposals together. Midway though this process, VISTA paid my way to a week-long seminar on grant writing. This enabled me to spend time in a nice hotel in Austin and to act like I knew what I was doing when I returned, even though I'd never written a grant proposal before in my life.

Once I developed a few ideas about how to use potential funds—a nutrition program, a new ventilation system (the old one was the culprit in my positive skin test for tuberculosis), a puppet show-based HIV and AIDS education program for children in elementary school—I set to work on researching local and national funding sources and putting proposals together. Going down to the funding library and researching private foundations wasn't especially fun. But I came to love the process of sitting down with different people at the foundation and in the community to talk about how to put a new program together. What would the dietitian do? Who would

I APPRECIATE YOUR HELP WITH THE "AIDS EDUCATION FOR KIDS" PROPOSAL, BUT A PUPPET DRAG SHOW MIGHT NOT FLY WITH THE P.T.A.....

design the puppets? How many air changes per hour would the new roof units provide?

In the end, the nutrition grant was funded, as was an HIV community education grant for a female-run barrio-based agency called the Mujeres Project. A grant for improving the ventilation system was funded, too. In all, my grants brought in $200,000 worth of new funding to the foundation.

Looking back, I realize that the real meaning in VISTA lies not so much in the tangible effects we may or may not have had on a community but in the education that we all gained in practical change. "Giving something back," we learned how to make our voices heard and how to respect people whose view of the world doesn't necessarily match ours. For me—and for lots of VISTA volunteers—the VISTA year isn't about attaining specific goals but rather about figuring out how to integrate broader goals into the next phase of your life.

Today I've kept my involvement in the struggle against AIDS by working part time for an annual conference on AIDS and Chinese medicine. I'm also in film school, making documentaries, which I attribute to my year with VISTA. My goal of exposing different parts of America to one another through film stems directly from the way VISTA uncovered communities for me. I will always be grateful for that incredibly rich and challenging experience.

Some Advice from Daniel

Surviving on a Pittance: Check into the cost of living in the place where your VISTA assignment is. Make sure it is possible to make ends meet on the monthly stipend. Rent in San Antonio was unbelievably cheap, which made $600 a month go a long way. In other places it might not be so easy.

Big City or Small Town: I originally had my heart set on working in a small town, but in retrospect I'm really glad I was in a place where there were lots of other recent-graduate VISTAs. Being the only one would have made it difficult to keep going during the periods of frustration.

When to Arrive: If you can manage it, it's a good idea to arrive in your new community a week or two early. This way you'll have time to find a place to live and settle in before the preservice orientation.

Being Flexible: Some people have to wait months before their VISTA assignment comes through. Being flexible about what kind of location you want tends to speed things up. I originally wanted to volunteer in Kentucky, where I grew up, but rather than wait around for another couple of months or more, I grabbed the San Antonio opportunity when it came along.

Getting Along with Agency Staff: VISTAs can find themselves in the awkward situation of being assigned to do work that overlaps with the job description of employees at their agencies. It is certainly not unheard of for agency employees or even directors to feel threatened by the presence of full-time volunteers from outside the community. Be conscious of your position as an "outsider" and the dynamics that could result from that and attempt not to step on others' toes.

A Few Resources to Help You Out

AmeriCorps VISTA (1201 New York Avenue NW, Washington, D.C. 20525, [800] 424-8867). The objective of this one-year program is to help individuals with low incomes improve conditions in their lives. Instead of providing direct services, volunteers work as organizers and catalysts to "help make things happen." Call for an information packet.

Who Cares: A Journal of Service and Action (1511 K Street NW, Suite 1042, Washington, D.C. 20005, [800] 628-1692). Recently established by four young college graduates, this highly acclaimed magazine offers honest articles and helpful resources on community service and nonprofit work. It's written for and by our generation. You may find it in your career center or at a well-stocked bookstore. Call for subscription information.

Good Works: A Guide to Careers in Social Justice, ed. Jessica Cowan (New York: Barricade Books, 1993). Offers profiles on over eight hundred groups involved in social change. The comprehensiveness of this listing and the employment information included makes it an excellent resource for anyone interested in working in the nonprofit sector.

Community Jobs: The Employment Newspaper for the Non-Profit Sector (ACCESS: Networking in the Public Interest, 30 Irving Place, Ninth Floor, New York, N.Y. 10003, [212] 475-1001). This paper has job listings organized by region and state that provide job descriptions, salaries, and necessary qualifications. The cost is $29 for a three-month subscription and $39 for six months.

The National Service Guide: How You Can Find Opportunities to Make a Difference (New York: ACCESS: Networking in the Public Interest, 1994). This reference guide lists service corps and volunteer centers nationwide, as well as resources for finding jobs and internships in the nonprofit sector. You can order it for $5 plus $1.95 shipping and handling from ACCESS: Networking in the Public Interest, 30 Irving Place, Ninth Floor, New York, N.Y. 10003, (212) 720-5627.

Working in

Washington

Alexandra Robert

From stumbling over the Pledge of Allegiance in kindergarten to debating U.S. Latin American policy in some senior seminar, you've probably been talking about politics for years. Now might be your chance to become more involved, by becoming part of a political campaign, doing research for a policy think tank, working as an intern on Capitol Hill, or perhaps even being a political speechwriter, which is exactly what Alexandra did.

"So, how did you get into speechwriting?" someone will ask.

"Serendipity," I always reply.

As a little girl I wanted to be a large assortment of characters: a princess, a firefighter, a chicken, the president, my dad. Never once did I imagine becoming a speechwriter. And, unlike a select cadre who have degrees in rhetoric and/or umpteen years of political experience, I had never done anything in my life that could be called direct preparation for this craft.

Actually, I had never done anything in my young life that could be called direct preparation for *any* craft. I was *pre*-preprofessional. I had, until recently, suffered what Calvin Trillin has called "Provisional Life Syndrome"—an unwillingness to "get on track," a reluctance to start becoming the woman I want to be after my fifteen-year reunion from college.

I kept hoping that if I remained productive and honorable, God would reward me with a long-term plan. It didn't happen.

Sometime after graduation, I decided to move to Washington, D.C. The year was 1993 and I had an acute case of Clinton fever. After many years, change seemed possible, and I wanted to be a part of it. Unfortunately, so did many young people who had an advantage over me: they had worked on the campaign.

"You are not going to get a job in this administration," I was told repeatedly. "While you were getting all bright and shiny, lots of other people your age were on the campaign trail. Some of them even dropped out of college to work for Clinton-Gore."

I refused to be dissuaded. I sat through endless informational interviews, sent innumerable résumés and cover letters, watched a lot of daytime television, took part-time jobs, and prayed. And then I met my fairy godmother. Ellen does not have a magic wand. She has a faculty position at Barnard College and ten years of experience in politics. I told her what I wanted to do.

"You probably won't get a job in this administration," she began. By this time I had developed the skill of seeming to listen while singing "La-la-la-la" over and over inside my head.

"Unless . . ."

I stopped singing. "Unless what?!"

"Unless . . . can you write?"

I thought of the untold cover letters, essays, my honors thesis. "Sure, I can write."

I sent Ellen a writing sample, which she sent to two friends, who sent it to two friends, and so on. My résumé traveled a long and circuitous route (that I do not think I could reproduce) and some-how landed on the desk of the chief of staff to First Lady Hillary Rodham Clinton. It might have laid there for months except the first lady's speechwriter was nine months pregnant with twins and dangerously close to her maternity leave. Like most people in gov-ernment, those of the Office of the First Lady had little time or inclination for advance planning. And so, on the day my résumé arrived, they were quite desperate. I was young, I was eager, I could write. They were going to give me a chance.

IN THE WHITE HOUSE

This seems no less incredible to me now than it did a year and a half ago, when, having carefully followed the directions I had been given, I found myself standing in front of the White House. I stood there for a while just looking through the gates, taking it in, dumbstruck and misty-eyed. When I say I was overwhelmed, I don't just mean that I was scared, which I was; I mean that I was overcome by feelings as powerful as they are ineffable.

I kept waiting for someone to stop me, to tell me I had no business being there, except everyone seemed to think that I did. I was asked to write a speech on health care for the first lady to deliver to the Union of American Hebrew Congregations and given a deadline just three days away.

I spent the first day reading speeches the first lady had given and learning about the Clinton health care plan. I spent the second wishing I had paid closer attention in Hebrew school and researching Maimonides, the Torah, and any piece of Judaica that could be relevant. The third day was spent writing and rewriting, working to make pages of scribbled notes into awe-inspiring oratory.

There was no time to panic, but I did anyway. And then it was finished. Well, provisionally finished. Any big speech will be edited, vetted, and, as we say in our less charitable moments, "big footed" by several higher powers, usually the chief of staff, the relevant policy people, and, finally, the principal—in this case, Hillary Rodham Clinton.

"What's she like?" people always ask. I am forced to disappoint by admitting that I really do not know. Here was my first revelation about speechwriting: one does not necessarily know (in any meaningful sense) the person for whom they write. Former speechwriter Peggy Noonan wrote for President Reagan for several months before she met him. I wrote countless sets of remarks for more than two months before I had even a photo opportunity with Mrs.

Clinton. In the four months I worked at the White House, I spoke to her twice.

I did speak *through* her, though. It was an incredible high to hear the first lady vocalize my words or to see phrases I had written quoted in the newspaper. It was less thrilling to read transcripts of speeches that bore absolutely no resemblance to the ones I had written.

Some government officials read their texts verbatim. These are not the people for whom I have written. Since leaving the White House—after Mrs. Clinton's regular speechwriter weaned herself from the twins—I have been speechwriter to a cabinet secretary who has been known to begin speeches by saying, "You know I have some very talented people working for me, and they've prepared a great speech for me to give tonight, but I left it at home because I'm just going to speak candidly."

This is when I wonder why I wasted an hour searching for a really great Harry Truman quote and deciding whether to say "quickly" or "rapidly."

Speechwriting—and working for the government—does have its fair share of frustrations: your research material often comes to you (late) in the impenetrable code of "bureaucratese"; people rarely agree on the substance of a speech and it is up to you to write a text that will satisfy everyone and still say something more meaningful than "Human rights—good"; and finally, it is difficult to watch your ideals founder on the shores of political reality.

POLITICAL LOOKS

There is a special look that seasoned political animals reserve for upstarts like myself. This barely perceptible freezing of the jaw and a slight lift of the eyebrow means "You just don't understand." And during my first six months on the job with the cabinet secretary, I got this look a lot.

"I'm a little bit puzzled by something," I said one day in a fairly high-level meeting. "I keep writing that every billion dollars of

exports creates twenty thousand jobs . . . but this isn't a net figure. I mean, what about all the jobs we are losing through free trade?"

Jaws tightened. Eyebrows lifted. I have since written "every billion dollars of exports creates twenty thousand U.S. jobs" one hundred times as penance.

I have also developed a new look of my own. It's called "Well, I understand that, but . . . ," and I use it selectively. It is a discerning smile that says, Of course I have to write whatever you tell me, even if it as repugnant as what you just said, but just listen here a moment.

To smile like this takes nerve. As a beginner, confronting political hacks and policy wonks and saying "I disagree" and/or "Here is my view" is both a courageous and an audacious act. You may be setting yourself up to hear, "When I was as young and idealistic as you are now, I thought that, too," or reminded that bright-eyed does not necessarily mean bright.

Thankfully, this rarely happens. More often than not, the response is positive. That doesn't mean those of us lower down on the political food chain make the final decisions. The speechwriters, the legislative aides, the special assistants do not set policy. We do not determine communications strategy. C-SPAN and CNN are not beating down our doors. No one is going to interrupt a meeting to take my call. But they will probably call me back. And more often than not, they will consider what I have to say.

PART OF THE PROCESS

Even if some animals in government are more equal than others, each of us derives significant value—and I think ample satisfaction—from being part of a larger whole. Certainly there are days when it is very easy to get mired in minutia, days when I feel like a glorified typist. I know there are days when colleagues of mine feel that if they could spend as much time thinking as faxing and performing mindless administrative tasks, they could probably discover a way to balance the federal budget without cutting a single social program.

But there are also days when everything comes together. Days when endless small details become successful negotiations with a foreign government or a series of development grants for impoverished communities. These are the days that I think of Washington, D.C., as Our Nation's Capital. These are the days I see through all of the red tape and I remember why I came here.

I came to be a part of the process, and I am. Unlike many an intern who believes he or she is single-handedly responsible for the passage of the crime bill, I know my role is small. But I belong here. Should I choose to take it, there is a place for me. At least until the next election.

Jobs in politics are not for the faint of heart. They are not for those who crumble under deadline pressure and election insecurity, or for those who fear the photocopier, fax, and phone. Ultimately they may not be for me.

Still, I do know that this is where I overcame "Provisional Life Syndrome." I have not made a full recovery, but I do have an outline of a long-term plan. Oddly, putting words in other people's mouths has helped me to define my own.

Come autumn I will be carrying my own weight in law books and waxing nostalgic about the good ol' days in D.C. Every time I watch the State of the Union Address, I will feel sorry for the speechwriters who have spent days without sleep. When one of my school friends is bemoaning some breach of idealism, it is likely that my jaw will tighten and my eyebrows will lift. You just don't understand, I will say. You don't realize what we are up against. Sometimes I will watch the news and, fully aware of political realities, my lips will curl in a discerning smile and I will be certain that I am right and the experts are wrong.

Some Advice from Alexandra

Being Here Now: While you can do some preliminary research before you arrive, the truth is it's difficult to find work in Washington unless you're *in* Washington. Political jobs come and go quickly. Being there gives you a better shot at being in the right place at the right time.

Working on a Campaign: If you think you might be interested in working in politics, here is your trial by fire. Everyone whom I have met who worked on a campaign describes it as an incredible and incomparable experience. If your candidate wins, you have a good shot at a staff position. If he or she loses, you have still (most likely) made invaluable contacts and "paid your dues."

Getting an Internship: Again, this is an excellent way to make contacts and gain experience. It's also a good way to see what an organization is like without making a long-term commitment. Unfortunately, internships rarely pay much, if anything at all.

Networking: If politics is not about who you know, then it's about *whom* you know. And even though I find it kind of distasteful and embarrassing, networking is necessary. Start with the people you know. Get the names of their contacts and phone them. Get the contacts of the contacts and phone them. Have your contacts phone them. Jobs often come from the strangest places. I am not saying you need to become a craven and rabid self-promoter, but you do need to be assertive.

Knowing What Makes You So Special: Something you take for granted, such as your ability to write or your knowledge of statistics, may make you quite marketable in government. Highlight this in your interviews and/or résumé.

Timing and Burnout: Most jobs in politics are intense and the burnout factor is pretty high. The average tenure of a political apointee is eighteen months. A year is considered respectable.

Insecurity: This seems like an obvious fact, but since so many politicos have blocked it from their minds, I will state it plainly: politics does not offer great job security. There is the potential for congressional turnover every two years. If the senator for whom you work returns to the private sector, she usually does not take you with her. Try to keep your options open and some emergency money in the bank.

A Few Resources to Help You Out

Senate Placement Office (Hart Office Building, Room 142, Washington, D.C. 20510, [202] 224-9167). This organization serves as a résumé referral service for the U.S. Senate. It receives requests from committee offices and senators with staff openings and matches the requests with people in its files.

House Placement Office (219 Ford House Office Building, Third and D Street SW, Washington, D.C. 20515, [202] 226-6731). This organization plays a role similar to the Senate Placement Office but for the House of Representatives.

Jobs in Washington DC: 1001 Great Opportunities for College Graduates, by Greg Diefenbach and Philip Giordano (Manassas Park, Va.: Impact Publications, 1992). This is a good starting place for Washington job leads both inside and outside of politics. It is made up of an extensive organization list, peppered with in-depth profiles.

Congressional Quarterly's Washington Information Directory (Washington, D.C.: Congressional Quarterly, 1995). This one-thousand-plus-page reference tomb is probably not something you'll want to buy and lug home, but it is worth tracking down at a career center or library. Broken down by broad fields—law and justice, health, international affairs, and so forth—it provides useful job-hunting information about the various public, private, and nonprofit organizations in the Washington area.

Federal Jobs for College Graduates, by Robert Goldenkoff and Dana Morgan (New York: Prentice Hall, 1991). Includes information on various federal agencies and describes jobs available. The data is concise, but the range of job listings is comprehensive.

Going Back for More

What do you do if you've come to the end of the academic road and you're still hungry for more? Or suppose you spend a couple of years out in the "real world" and find you need more credentials to do what you want to do?

Maybe you should head back to graduate school.

The reasons people return are as disparate as the range of graduate programs available. For some, the draw is academic curiosity—perhaps you've cultivated an interest in urban planning, the decline of the Mayan civilization, or Colonial American literature, and you'd like the opportunity to pursue it further. For others, graduate school is a means to an appealing end—a way to be able to fulfill a desire to practice medicine, become a lawyer, teach in a public school, or enter a field where your bachelor's degree won't hold weight against the advanced degrees of other job seekers. And for some, graduate school is simply a safe haven that provides them a little more time to figure out what's next.

The problem is, without actually taking the plunge, it can be hard to figure out whether the substantial time and financial commitment involved in going to graduate school is actually worthwhile. So to help you out, this section offers a few thoughts from those who have already returned to school. If you've ever thought about medical school, law school, getting a master's, or even pursuing a Ph.D., here's your chance to get an inside look.

Getting a

Master's Degree

Susan Friedland

You've dabbled in everything from art history to post-Freudian psychology, but how much is that worth in the real world? Would it make sense to go back and earn a degree in a focused master's program? Here are a few thoughts on what that experience is like.

Contrary to popular belief, graduate students don't just roll their own cigarettes and quote Foucault. Although graduate school may not be the "real world," for me, getting a master's degree in city planning has been a chance to focus on acquiring concrete skills I could apply outside academia. It also allowed me to make a detour from a career trajectory I was racing through without much reflection. It was an opportunity to meet intelligent and motivated people, of different ages and backgrounds, who all shared my passion for urban issues. And, of course, there was still plenty of time to sit in cafés in the middle of the day, rolling cigarettes while pondering the meaning of life.

After a two-year stint in the working world, I realized that if I was really serious about making the world a better place, I needed to arm myself with every possible tool. I couldn't rely on my good intentions alone but needed to be able to think like a real estate developer, read plans like an architect, and crunch numbers like an accountant. Although I have had to overcome my liberal-artsy phobia of numbers and disdain for business, I have remained committed to my principles. It's a great thing to have good intentions, but it's even better to be able to carry them out.

Professional master's programs come in all stripes, from public health to forestry to business administration. I chose city planning for some practical reasons as well as for some romantic ones. I wanted to learn about the policies and theories that shaped the urban world around me. What *are* enterprise zones and can they work? How are land-use decisions made? How is low-income housing financed? That's the policy wonk side of me. But in my heart, I have simply always loved the fabric of cities—old brick warehouses, tiny well-worn urban parks, neighborhood groceries, huge modern towers. From the many courses I had taken in college, the ones that dealt with urban issues, policies, and architecture had interested me the most. I knew graduate school would allow me to revisit many of these topics in more intellectually sophisticated and empirical ways.

A Day in the Life of a Grad Student

Certain aspects of my life as a graduate student mirrored undergraduate life. I could still wake up at 8:45 A.M., pull on my torn jeans, stuff my hair in a baseball cap, and stumble into my 9:30 class. I could work whenever I felt productive, even at the oddest and most unpredictable hours. I could also enjoy all of the perks of being associated with a university and have access to free resources that can cost a bundle in the outside world—such as a gym and an E-mail account. On the flip side, of course, I was still haunted by that pesky feeling that there was always more reading to be done.

But aside from these few things, graduate school was a remarkably different experience from college. Scary as it may sound, I found myself becoming more serious about my work and myself. Unlike in college, where we ran around trying to acquire general knowledge of every topic from Japanese poetry to modern European history, in graduate school I now knew what I wanted to learn. My classmates shared this focus, because for many of us, graduate school was a big investment of our time and money. Most of my peers had come to graduate school with several years of work experience under their belts. Among them were former policy analysts, college admissions officers, landscape architects, environmental organizers, journalists, even one theater director. All of us wanted to be involved in some aspect of city planning. None of us could really afford to slack off or remain indecisive in a fast-paced two-year program.

My relationships with professors were closer than they had been in college. But even though I could now call a professor by his or her first name, this is not to say that I would go to his or her house for tea and heart-to-heart conversations. For the most part, my professors tended to be hurried and overcommitted. However, when I approached them with concrete ideas or questions, they would generally offer good critiques of my work or put me in touch with helpful people outside of school.

By the time I got to graduate school, I had stopped worrying about grades. I felt that classes were my chance to learn, not to perform according to a certain standard. In a way that I might have been too cautious to do in college, I often raised controversial questions or asked for clarification. Sometimes I would watch a professor grimace or sigh at a question or comment, but I felt vindicated when other students would approach me after class and admit that they wished they had raised the same question. In the end, those same professors whom I had challenged became my most trusted advisers.

The Classes

Comparing graduate courses to college, I found that the quantitative classes had the greatest overlap. Formulas on the blackboard, textbooks, problem sets, final exams, and those dreaded moments of complete lack of comprehension all brought back memories of my undergraduate experience. Fortunately, my program fostered a very cooperative and noncompetitive environment, so those of us without a clue in statistics could hover around the department computer room and seek help from the numerically enlightened.

Seminars in graduate school tend to be more animated. I rarely experienced that deadly silence that comes when no one has done the reading and everyone just stares blankly at the professor. For the most part, discussions were lively and rooted in students' personal and professional experiences. In one session of an economic development class, a group of students who had just met with city planners in Los Angeles gave a presentation of the Crips' and Bloods' joint plan to regenerate their neighborhoods. This is something you would never find in a textbook.

Studios were a new and intense experience. There were several possible options offered each semester—urban design, housing development, transportation planning, community planning. For my housing development studio, we worked with a real client to create a low-income housing development plan for a tiny, affluent bedroom community nearby. This client, a local nonprofit-housing developer, was interested not only in our actual architectural designs but also in our research into the income levels and housing needs of the community; the types of housing that already exist; how we would finance the project; and how we would gain political approval for the project.

Six weeks later we had to make a presentation, requiring us to strategize, work together, and complete the project as a group. I had never really liked working in groups in college, as I felt that certain people always ended up doing more than their share of the work. In graduate school it was the complete opposite. Even in moments of last-minute hysteria, when the architects were frantically trying to coach the community organizers on ways to shade in trees on the final drawings, there was a sense of professional collaboration and exhilaration at working successfully as a team. Watching my teammates pull off a spectacular presentation the next day gave me a great sense of shared accomplishment, even though the trees turned out a bit lopsided.

This sense of community and closeness with my classmates is something that is easily fostered in master's programs, which are generally small and intense. We shared more than just classes together. We spent countless hours talking about our aspirations, complaining about course work, hanging out in the shabby student lounge, helping one another find jobs, and, eventually, calling one another from our new jobs. This group continues to provide a social and professional network.

OUTSIDE THE CLASSROOM

Like most of my classmates, I worked part time during graduate school. Scholarships and grants are hard to come by for master's students, yet opportunities for internships and paid projects are plentiful and are a great way to gain professional experience. Three afternoons a week, I labored over spreadsheets in a nonprofit bank in order to earn a paycheck as well as the financial skills that I would need after graduation. Other classmates planned public health conferences, organized neighborhoods to plant trees, held workshops for community planning, wrote freelance articles, worked in city government offices, and even performed in dance concerts.

Unlike my first year out of college, my transition from life as a graduate student to "real life" was not a traumatic one. First of all, I was confident that I had skills an employer might actually need. My classmates and I had learned how to effectively put together a housing plan for a city or design an infrastructure system or run participatory community meetings. I was also encouraged by the great variety of contacts I made with people and organizations over the course of my two years. But mostly, all of us helped one another out, sharing job listings and names. In the end, everyone in our graduating class found jobs.

As I think back on my two years in graduate school, I can think of some singularly amazing experiences, like leading a city-planning workshop with urban high schoolers and feeling their excitement build as they began to talk about solving problems in their own neighborhoods. What I remember most are not the specific details of problem set number eight but the general sense of confidence that I could do whatever I set my mind to.

Ironically, I am back in school again. At eight o'clock every morning before work, I sit in a small classroom with undergraduates and speak in faltering Russian. I need to learn Russian because one of the professors who used to groan at my questions has offered me a job. Soon I will be off to work for the city of St. Petersburg, doing economic development.

This is what going back to school is all about—learning and opening your life to limitless possibilities. Graduate school gave me the opportunity to strive for a meaningful balance between thought and practice. In my mind, skills without idealism makes just a technocrat while idealism without real world skills makes merely a dreamer.

Some Advice from Susan

GETTING TO GRADUATE SCHOOL

Your Essay: Although you may not be totally clear on exactly why you are going to graduate school, your entrance application essay needs to be focused and specific. As you probably know, the world does not deal well with ambiguity. Keep it short and to the point. Use concrete examples of what you can bring to the program and what you want to learn.

Your Application: This is your chance to stand out from the crowd. Be sure to send in any examples of reports or other projects you have worked on. If you wrote a senior thesis and it's relevant, send it. Also, you may want to submit more letters of recommendation than is required, especially from professionals in your field.

Visit the Department: If at all possible, visit the campus to meet with professors and talk to students. This will help you get a sense of what you like or do not like about a department. It can also give your name a face in the application process. A positive note in your application from a professor you happen to meet during your visit can really help.

WHILE IN GRADUATE SCHOOL

Making the Most of Your Time: If you are attending a master's program in a big university, don't limit yourself to the classes in your department. Take advantage of other related fields that may give you complementary knowledge or skills.

Don't Worry Too Much About Grades: If you aren't planning to go for a doctorate, you will never need to get into school again. Equally important, employers almost never ask about your grad school GPA. And as if that weren't enough, grades tend to be inflated in graduate programs anyway. Chances are, if you try, you will do fine, so don't waste your education worrying about it.

Working: If you need to work, and I recommend it as a way to get professional experience, try to keep your work and your academic schedules separate. Set your time in the office as work time and your time at school as academic time. You can drive yourself crazy otherwise. If you have the opportunity, try to find a teaching assistant position. This might be your only chance to teach. Even if you decide you never want to stand in front of a class again, it is a great way to see what being a professor is like and to develop close relationships with undergraduates. It also pays well and lets you stay on campus.

Don't Be Afraid to Treat Yourself Well: Graduate school is one of those places where people don't pat you on the back too often. To the extent that you can, choose projects and paper topics of interest to you personally. Find professors to work with who are known to be nice and supportive people—there is really no reason to work with a jerk, even a famous jerk. Make time for yourself to do the things that you love and that provide an escape from the halls of your department. Get a dog.

Getting a Job: While in school, make use of the resources available to you and be creative about finding some that aren't apparent. Talk to alumni, attend conferences, pick your classmates' brains. Another thing to do: take time to make all of your papers, especially your final project, relevant to your field and presentable. Often you will be able to find an organization that needs a project done and a professor who will give you credit for it. Those projects are great to bring around to job interviews.

A Few Resources to Help You Out

Graduate Admissions Essays: What Works, What Doesn't and Why, by Donald Asher (Berkeley, Calif.: Ten Speed Press, 1991). Offers suggestions for how to develop a persuasive essay, numerous samples of essays that are effective, and a couple of examples of essays that are ineffective.

Graduate Record Examinations: Educational Testing Service (P.O. Box 6000, Princeton, N.J. 08541-6000, [609] 771-7670). If you're going to pursue a master's degree, you need to take the Graduate Record Examinations (GRE), offered five times a year—usually in February, April, June, October, and December. Pick up a registration booklet at your college career center or call or write the office directly.

Princeton Review (2315 Broadway, New York, N.Y. 10024, [800] 333-0369). One of the two big test-prep organizations. It offers a five-week

GRE-preparation course for $745. Call for more information and to get the location of the office nearest you.

Kaplan Educational Centers (810 Seventh Avenue, 22d Floor, New York, N.Y. 10019, [212] 492-5990). This is the other test-prep giant. It offers a five-week GRE-preparation course for $695. Call for information and office locations.

For other resources, see "Getting a Ph.D.," page 192.

Artists in

Medical

Wonderland

Sayantani DasGupta

**What happens when you mix a free-spirited, creative thinker with
the rigor and discipline of medical school? You'll probably end up
with an inquisitive and slightly exasperated medical student who
will ultimately become a damn good doctor. At least that's what
Sayantani hopes.**

"Mrs. Johnson is a seventy-two-year-old African-American woman
admitted to the Johns Hopkins hospital for the first time last Tuesday," I recited in the most bland monotone I could muster, desper-
ately attempting to straightjacket years of dramatic training into
the dry, flat style of the medical patient presentation. Keeping my
eyes riveted on the third button of my instructor's white coat, I
continued, "With a chief complaint of not being able to dance."

"Excuse me, Miss DasGupta? Perhaps I didn't hear the chief
complaint correctly."

I imagined the elderly physician's bald head beading up with
perspiration, his bow tie dancing agitatedly. Perhaps this was not
the appropriate time to tell him that I preferred to be called *Ms.*
DasGupta.

"Mrs. Johnson's chief complaint is that she can't dance," I explained to the third button. "She has some degree of left leg muscle atrophy, but it's not really affecting her lifestyle except that she can't dance anymore."

"As a physician, whether or not a seventy-two-year-old woman can dance is not of primary concern," announced Dr. Meanie authoritatively. "Perhaps it would behoove you to conceptualize her disease in more medically relevant terminology."

I thought of the lovely, grandmotherly patient I had just interviewed. Her daughter-in-law, clearly frustrated by the burdens of caring for an elderly relative, had brought Mrs. Johnson in on the presumed excuse that she was showing signs of early Alzheimer's— babbling on and on about not being able to dance. But during my subsequent patient interview, I soon realized that Mrs. Johnson wasn't delusional, or senile, or even unreasonable.

"Honey," she explained, her clear brown eyes warm and expressive, "I just ain't been myself since my leg gave out. . . . Every night, I used to turn on them records my husband and I used to listen to and dance and dance . . . but now, I tell my leg to move and it don't. It ain't the same since I can't dance no more."

As someone who regularly shuts all the doors and windows and dances by herself to everything from Ali Akbar Khan to the Crash Test Dummies, I could empathize with Mrs. Johnson's problem. Whether or not my instructor agreed, the biggest impediment to Mrs. Johnson's well-being was her inability to dance—and in my mind, that, more than any biochemically defined, anatomically pinpointable disease process, was what was impinging on her health. Even though "inability to dance" is not in the great holy book of medicine, the *Physician's Desk Reference*, maybe it should be. And maybe I'll be the one to put it there.

A "NEW MEDICINE"

There is a new aesthetic of medicine emerging in this country. This aesthetic, shaped by such diverse forces as governmental reform, the HIV-AIDS epidemic, and a renewed interest in traditional and holistic systems of health care, redefines our ideas of health, disease, and what it means to be a physician. While an intangible phenomenon, this idea of "new medicine" is being recognized by even such traditional old-boys-network institutions as Johns Hopkins Medical School. When I, a self-defined "humanities person" who focused in college on writing, drama, feminist theory, and anthropology, arrived at Hopkins, I soon realized that even this mecca of basic science research has been affected by the power of new medicine. Indeed, within my entering class of 120, Hopkins actively recruited a number of nontraditional medical students, covert premeds with backgrounds in everything from French literature to architecture. I even know one ex-sculptor whose love of the human form inspired him to aim for a career as a surgeon.

"You are future physicians, not just scientists, but artists . . . and your palette is humanity," pontificated one of the deans during our welcoming address. "Just remember, it will be you who brings new life into this world . . . and oftentimes, your face will be the last sight someone sees before they close their eyes forever."

I'm a little embarrassed to say that I was moved to tears by this blatantly melodramatic speech, which was probably pinched directly from a script of "Chicago Hope" or "St. Elsewhere." In the two years since that welcoming address, I have realized that despite the recruitment of nontraditional (read "non-lab-rat") students, Johns Hopkins remains a fairly traditional institute of medicine. Yet when I arrived at Hopkins, I didn't know my way out of a test tube, and the "St. Elsewhere" speech was an enormous reassurance. More important, it was an acknowledgment of the amorphous ideas about social change, being an artist and a scientist, and caring for people's holistic health that had propelled me into medicine. The fact that I, a prototypic humanities student who knew substantially more about feminist theory, postmodern playwrights, and South Asian history than about biology, chemistry, or physics, was accepted to be a Johns Hopkins medical student says a lot in and of itself about the changing face of medicine.

ARTISTS IN WONDERLAND

The art of medicine was once exactly that—an art, complete with personal interpretations, varied styles, unique visions and rhythms. However, modern technology and the essentialization of Western medical knowledge has transformed the healing art into something very much resembling the art of plumbing: pipe A into pipe B, screw that rivet there. For a humanities-educated student entering medical school, the sheer discipline of memorizing a lot of facts, sitting in long hours of lecture, and being evaluated through objective exams rather than creative papers is often quite a shock. For me, coming to medical school was like learning an entirely new language and vision of the world. No longer could I just ramble endlessly in class without having done the reading—I actually needed to substantiate what I said in scientific fact. Even more alien was the lack of autonomy. While I designed my own papers, assignments, and even course topics in college, I was forced to study exactly what I was told to study in medical school. It was more than a rude awakening.

The first two years of medical school, which are based on lecture and textbook learning, are often about memorizing a lot of intricate anatomic physiologic, pharmacologic, and pathologic details. This period can be the most difficult time for those of us who come to medical school with a liberal arts background. Not only are we unfamiliar with most of the information being presented, but we are oftentimes shocked at the long lecture hours, the noninteractive, noncreative learning style, the need to memorize rather than analyze. The other day I was griping about this very subject to a pathophysiology professor when he asked me what I would like to see changed about my medical school curriculum. While I had some concrete suggestions about fewer class hours and more creative learning, I soon realized that the first two years of medical school are perhaps a necessary evil. There is an enormous amount of information that students don't know but must know before they become physicians in charge of people's health.

The bright side of two years of memorizing minutia comes during the third and fourth years, when medical students are in the hospital

actually caring for patients. During this second half of medical training, students are required to rotate through various disciplines for anywhere from two to nine weeks. Pediatrics, obstetrics/gynecology, surgery, psychiatry, neurology, opthamology, emergency medicine—each one in turn will become your life, consuming most of your waking day. Some rotations are required. Some are elective experiences students can choose—opting for further training within their own institution or at other institutions across the country or around the world. The freedom to partially design your education and to schedule breaks and vacations to your own liking is part of the charm of these years. It is during this time that most "nontraditional" medical students shine, since it is in the hospital that students must think creatively and on their feet, interacting with and extracting information from the wide variety of patients who enter a hospital. As someone just beginning the second half of my medical education, I am already feeling the relief of escaping from the classroom and two years of socializing with the same 120 students.

Indeed, while the first two years of basic sciences often made me feel inadequate and doubtful of my future in medicine, early experiences in the hospital have reaffirmed my career decision.

For the artist in medical wonderland, medicine is an open-ended career defined by possibilities rather than limitations. An M.D. degree can lead to careers in anything from academic medicine, research, or private practice to medical-legal issues, medical ethics, public health, or health policy. While I worry about the time constraints of medicine, the struggles of raising a family, and the traditionally woman-unfriendly history of the medical profession, I also recognize the changes in modern medicine and the redefinition of what it means to be a physician and healer. I am ultimately glad I left the secure environment of liberal arts academe for the unfamiliar territory of the medical wonderland. It is here that I believe I can effect the most change, both with the knowledge I gather and within the institutions from which I gather it.

A Leap of Faith

There are a significant and growing number of students who come to the wonderland of medical school from a very different place. They take this journey not necessarily for the love of science but because of varied, unique visions of what they will do with the knowledge they acquire in medical training. Many nontraditional medical students don't exactly know where their leap of faith will land them. As a philosopher from my long-ago liberal arts past once said, "The path will emerge as you walk it."

Some Advice from Sayantani

A FEW GOOD REASONS TO CONSIDER MEDICAL SCHOOL
I Want to Change the World: Goofy as it may sound, this is actually not a bad reason. Health care is one of the most basic and important human rights. By being a physician, you can also be a social activist. Most important, your activism is in a much-needed, tangible form. Organiza-

tions such as Amnesty International and Physicians for Social Welfare are good resources to consult.

I Want to Travel: Another good reason. International health is a burgeoning field. Emergency medicine, family practice, and infectious disease are among some of the more promising medical specialities that can provide people the opportunity to work abroad. As a physician, the opportunity to work in different countries is always a possibility. Resources to find out more about medicine and travel include organizations such as the World Health Organization and the Flying Doctors.

I Am a People Person: The most important skill to being a physician is perhaps the ability to relate and listen to people. As the discipline of medicine grows away from a solely technological field, the nature of the physician returns to its original, humanitarian form. Being a good listener is crucial not only to making proper diagnoses but to helping people heal themselves.

I Want a Challenge: For nontraditional students headed for medical school, science and math may be daunting subjects. Part of the reason I came to medical school, ironically, was because science *didn't* come naturally to me and I was sick and tired of being intimidated by it.

I Am Dedicated to a Particular Issue: Poignant examples of issue-oriented decisions to enter medical school have to do with the HIV-AIDS epidemic. As the most powerful new force to impact the health of the modern world, HIV and AIDS have inspired many whose lives have been touched by the disease to enter medicine.

A Few Not-So-Good Reasons to Consider Medical School

Delusions of Fame, Fortune, or Power: Medical school is incredibly expensive. You will remain in debt through four years of school as well as the three to twelve years you will spend as a resident often making less than minimum wage. There are much faster ways to become a big spender.

Because Someone Else Wants You To: Most of getting through medical school has to do with willpower and inspiration—two things only you can bring to it. While your friends and family may have good intentions, they don't want you to be miserable. And that is exactly what you would be if you entered the rigorous extravaganza of medical training to fulfill someone else's dream.

A FEW NOT-SO-GOOD EXCUSES
NOT TO CONSIDER MEDICAL SCHOOL

It's Hard: OK, so you've heard that med school is grueling, with long hours and lots of information? That's all true. Med school is hard. But so are most things that are of any value. While it is sometimes conceptually difficult, most of the rigor of medical school has to do with maintaining willpower, vision, and discipline. If you're there for the right reasons, these things will get you through.

It's Expensive: Agreed. This is a cold, hard, and ugly fact. However, most U.S. citizens have so many scholarship and low-interest-loan opportunities available to them that financing medical education is not a huge problem. The real problem is that most students carry an incredible amount of debt—some have up to $100,000 hanging over their heads by the time they leave school. I suggest speaking to your undergraduate premed adviser or getting information from the financial aid department at any medical school in which you are interested.

I Don't Have the Prerequisites or I'm Too Old: Nonsense! I recently heard about a twenty-two-year-old woman and her forty-five-year-old mother who are in medical school together. There are plenty of people who decide to go to medical school after pursuing other careers, interests, and educational fields. There are also postbaccalaureate premed programs designed for such people. As a twenty-four-year-old, I feel that the older students in my class have much more perspective, drive, and dedication due to their rich backgrounds.

It Will Stifle My Free Spirit: While I admit to having this sentiment myself at times, I suggest to you what a friend suggested to me: there aren't that many jobs nowadays in being a free spirit. Bite the bullet, my friend; you have to do something. Why not have it be something from which you will ultimately receive incredible satisfaction? There's nothing to say you can't still read poetry, attend palm readings, and burn incense in your free time.

It's Full of Nerds: Very, very true. However, there are a significant number of unique and varied people who are heading to med school these days.

A Few Resources to Help You Out

Becoming a Doctor: A Journey of Initiation in Medical School, by Melvin Konner, M.D. (New York: Penguin Books, 1987). This engaging story provides a vivid picture of medical school, focusing particularly on the intense adventures of third-year rotations. Highly recommended.

Association of American Medical Colleges (AAMC) Student Services (1776 Massachusetts Avenue NW, Washington, D.C. 20036-1989, [202] 828-0620). If you're interested in medical school but didn't take premed courses during college, don't despair. Colleges around the country offer postbaccalaureate premed programs for late bloomers like you. Call the AAMC to request a free state-by-state listing of these programs.

MCAT Program Office (P.O. Box 4056, Iowa City, Iowa 52243, [319] 337-1357). If you're going to go to medical school, you need to take the Medical College Admission Test (MCAT). The test is offered twice a year (usually in April and August). Either pick up a registration booklet at your college career center or call or write the office directly.

Princeton Review (2315 Broadway, New York, N.Y. 10024, [800] 333-0369). One of the two big test-prep organizations. It offers a nine-week MCAT-preparation course for $945. Call for more information and the location nearest you.

Kaplan Educational Centers (810 Seventh Avenue, 22d Floor, New York, N.Y. 10019, [212] 492-5990). This is the other test-prep giant. It offers an eight-week MCAT-preparation course for $895. Call for information and office locations.

Life in
Law School

Nathanael Cousins

Not sure what to do after school? Thinking the security of a professional degree may help? Perhaps going to law school might be the path to take. In this essay, Nathanael reveals the good, the bad, and the ugly of being a law student.

Curtly calling out my last name, the professor triggers an involuntary reaction throughout the room. Seventy-five heads swivel to face the back-row victim. My legs mechanically lift me to a standing position, but a desperate darkness slips into my head, overwhelms my ears, and silently smothers my brain.

"Could you repeat the question please?" I stammer.

The professor, with an exasperated snort, again asks me to identify the plaintiff.

How can I be so slow? The previous night I spent two hours reading and briefing the twenty pages of cases for this class. Before class I neurotically met with my study group to review my analysis. To top it all off, I know the question is an easy one.

After what feels like an eternity, but is probably only a matter of seconds, the answer comes to me. My classroom comrades exhale with empathy and relief.

When the bell rings, ending class and taking me out of the hot seat, a friend congratulates me for surviving the gladiator session under the Socratic method. Some students blitz to the library to begin studying for the next two-hour class. Others sneak off to the bookstore to invest hundreds of dollars in a security blanket of study aids, hornbooks, and commercial outlines. All of us can taste the common intellectual excitement, competition, loneliness, and panic of being a "one L," a student in the first year of law school.

TRIAL BY FIRE: THE FIRST YEAR

If you decide you want to be an attorney, there are many hurdles ahead of you. Getting into law school is not easy. Then you must decide what type of law you would like to practice. After three years of studying, you must pass a comprehensive state bar exam. Finally, you need to find a job.

However, for anyone who wants to be an attorney, the first year of law school is the most dramatic hurdle of all. Like a military boot camp, the first year is the proving ground. You learn the legal language of *torts*, *estoppel*, and *jurisdiction*. You master a new method of reading and analyzing cases and legal arguments. You make new friends and perhaps live in a new part of the country. Moreover, your grades from the first year determine whether you make law review (the student-run law journal), along with future job opportunities and prestigious judicial clerkships. But perhaps most important, you begin to "think like a lawyer," developing a thought process that you will use throughout the rest of law school and your life. This intellectual transformation can be simultaneously empowering and disorienting. While armed with a new mode of analysis and a vocabulary of legalese, some recent undergraduates miss their former intellectual creativity, diversity, and freedom.

DAILY LIFE AS A FIRST-YEAR

I arrived for law school orientation bracing myself with an emotional football helmet. I had heard about the horrors of law school from lawyer relatives, *The Paper Chase*, and Scott Turow's revered law school autobiography, *One-L*. I was prepared for the worst—screaming professors, studying all night, students who steal your notes—but I wasn't prepared for the reality of law school.

In many ways, daily life in law school is more similar to ninth grade than to college. There are lockers, bells ring every period, and you probably live off campus. Generally law students do not participate in as many extracurricular activities as do undergraduates. You spend more time studying.

The core curriculum is consistent at most law schools. In your first two years, you take courses in contracts, criminal law, property, civil procedure, torts, constitutional law, wills and trusts, and legal writing. After that you are free to choose from electives. For instance, you might take a seminar on literature and the law, a lecture on international business transactions, or a practice course in trial advocacy skills.

In your first year, you take all of your classes with the same group of fifty to one hundred students, called a "section." Your seat is assigned by the professor. Within a few months, the students in your section become a family you both love and hate, but know very well. In our section, one woman would twist every answer into a narrative about a lawsuit she had against her neighbor. Another student always added a socialist perspective to any discussion. The first couple who started dating within the section were the focus of gossip for weeks. With the Socratic method combined with small-group syndrome, there is no success in being shy.

Within the first-year section, unofficial study groups are born, grow, divide, and squirm about like amoebas in a biology lab. The purpose of a study group is to work with other students in order to help yourself. My study group of six students was born about one month into school. At first we shared all of our notes and assigned "experts" for each class to prepare a comprehensive outline. Later we studied and stressed together about exams for weeks on end. In retrospect, the best thing about our study group was that we occasionally escaped from law school together for a basketball game, a beer, or a movie.

Law students, especially in the first semester, spend hours preparing for each class. The biggest laugh our contracts professor received all year was when she told us to "take a few days off and enjoy the city, visit your friends," three weeks before exams. Of course it was good advice, but the entire section intended to study that Friday night and every other night until the final exam.

Everyone has his or her own theory on how best to prepare for law school exams. Test preparation is like trying to drink from a fire hose spraying at full velocity—you must be selective or you will drown from too much information. Within my study group, one student plotted to miss the last two weeks of class and spent the time memorizing cases from flashcards. Another friend in his first semester typed out four hundred pages of outlines and tried to memorize them all. Before long you discover that you can be more efficient with your time and energy.

DOWNSHIFT: SECOND AND THIRD YEARS

If the first year of law school scares you to death, the second year works you to death and the third year can bore you to death. The second year of law school features increased reading, time-consuming law review projects, and endless interviews with potential employers. (By landing a job for the summer after your second year, you can ideally secure yourself a full-time position following law school.) Fortunately, the second year lacks the anxiety of the first year.

Comparatively, there are very few requirements or anxieties in the third year of law school, unless you can't find a job. Almost all of my classmates used one of the semesters to intern with a judge. I spent the fall studying European Community law in the Netherlands.

WHO GOES TO LAW SCHOOL, WHEN, AND WHY

One of the attractions of law school is that no particular background is required. In my class there are doctors, architects, entrepreneurs, professional athletes, and engineers. Nevertheless, more than half of the students graduated from college within the previous two years. The most common undergraduate majors are political science and economics.

Students attend law school for numerous reasons. It is frequently noted that you can use your law degree in other fields, including journalism, public policy, public service, and teaching. However, you should beware the "golden handcuffs" of a legal education. The $25,000 to $75,000 of debt that you can incur is most easily paid off as an attorney, unless you have previous experience in another lucrative field.

The most depressing law students are those who attend because they could not think of any alternatives after college. I see them on sunny spring days staring forlornly out library windows. Law school is difficult enough for the motivated, but it can be three years of misery for the unsure.

Is it a good idea to go to law school straight from undergraduate work? As my constitutional law professor says, there is a simple answer to every difficult question, and it is wrong. Some students are burned out after college and simply need a break from school. One of the top students in my class taught skiing for a year before law school and it charged up his batteries. Others gain valuable work experience that will help prepare them for law school. Many of my classmates worked as paralegals in law firms or at political posts in Washington, D.C., while others joined the Peace Corps.

Of course, many students come straight from college and succeeded in law school and as attorneys. I took the Law School Admissions Test (LSAT) my senior year in college and split the summer between traveling and working in a small law firm. At the time I was confident in my desire to be an attorney and fearful of floundering jobless in the real world. I felt prepared to move on to the next level.

LAW SCHOOL HORRORS AND MYTHS

Law school is the subject of many exaggerated urban legends. First is the legend of the carnivorous, student-munching law professor.

In three years I have had some professors who are disorganized or boring, but never a professor who took pleasure in terrorizing students. In sum, my professors have been engaging and supportive.

Second is the legend of the back-stabbing law student. According to this legend, students hide books from one another and sabotage notes in order to stay on top of the grading curve. In reality, students are tired and grumpy during exams, but I have not witnessed any intentional sabotage.

Third is the legend of the professor who grades exams by throwing them down stairs. The exams that reach the bottom step receive an "A," the next step "B," and so forth. While grades can seem are true. First, there are not jobs for all law school graduates. Sadly, you can study for three more years and incur great debt but still not find a job.

Second, law school is uncomfortably competitive. This is caused by the fact that law students are naturally competitive and are constantly being evaluated against one another. Students are graded on a steep curve. In our first-year class, only 15 percent of the students received an "A" mark, while 30 percent receive a "C" or below.

Finally, law school is still school. You have to study and take exams and you don't get paid. Your Thanksgiving holiday is spoiled for at least one year, maybe three, because you should be studying.

Is It Worth It?

Reflecting on my decision to attend law school, I conclude that I did not know what to expect. Law school has at times been exhilarating, depressing, intense, and overwhelming. I feel that I have learned important things about myself through the challenges of law school. Perhaps most important, I still want to become a lawyer.

Some Advice from Nathanael

Finding Out What Class Is Really Like: Go to a law school and ask the admissions office if you can sit in on some first-year classes. Usually the professors are happy to let you sit in back.

Applying to Law School: Admission is based on your grades, experience, recommendations, and the LSAT standardized entrance test. In my opinion, it's a good idea to prepare for the LSAT by making the investment to enroll in one of the commercial study courses (see resources listed below).

Working in a Law Firm Before Law School: Many private firms hire recent college graduates as entry-level clerks or paralegals. These positions can offer you insights into the life of a lawyer and often pay competitively.

Stress your academic record and writing and research skills when applying.

Choosing a Law School: There is more to it than national ranking, but where you go to school is important to career success. Consider the quality of student life, class size, and job placement.

Taking Undergraduate Classes to Prepare You for Law School: Take classes that challenge and interest you. It is not necessary to take a "prelaw" curriculum. Any courses that develop your analytical and writing skills will help. Law schools need fewer political scientists and more engineers and comparative religion majors.

Utilizing Resources: Your best resources in law school are your professors. Unlike lecturers in gargantuan undergraduate courses, law professors expect to engage students outside of class. They may be intimidating, but professors can be very helpful with career and academic advice.

A Few Resources to Help You Out

Full Disclosure: Do You Really Want to Be a Lawyer? by Susan J. Bell (Princeton, N.J.: Peterson's Guides, 1992). This compendium of candid essays about what really goes on in law school and in the practice of law is highly recommended.

Law School Admission Council (Box 2000, 661 Penn Street, Newtown, Penn. 18940-0998, [215] 968-1001). If you're going to go to law school, you need to take the Law School Admissions Test (LSAT), which is offered four times a year—usually in February, June, September, and December. Pick up a registration booklet at your college career center or call or write the office directly.

Princeton Review (2315 Broadway, New York, N.Y. 10024, [800] 333-0369). One of the two big test-prep organizations. It offers a five-week LSAT-preparation course for $745. Call for more information and to get the location of the office nearest you.

Kaplan Educational Centers (810 Seventh Avenue, 22d Floor, New York, N.Y. 10019, [212] 492-5990). The other test-prep giant. It offers a five-week LSAT-preparation course for $795. Call for information and office locations.

Looking at Law School: A Student Guide from the Society of Law School Teachers, ed. Stephen Gillers (New York: Meridian Books/Penguin Group, 1990). Examines how to select a law school and finance a law school education. It also contains special chapters addressing the concerns of minorities, women, and lesbians and gays, as well as informative essays about the subject matter explored in law school.

One-L, by Scott Turow (New York: Warner Books, 1988). A chilling autobiographical look at what life can be like for a first-year law student.

Getting a Ph.D.

Monica Rico

Academia is something you're plenty familiar with by now, but have you ever thought about pursuing it as a career? If you've toyed with the idea, then Monica's story may be of interest to you. Now in her third year of a Ph.D. in history, she shares some candid thoughts about the scholarly life.

The British Library's reading room stretches out underneath a huge dome. Two floors of reference books circle the walls, and rows of desks radiate out from the center like the spokes of a wheel. Karl Marx wrote *Das Kapital* sitting at one of these desks, I reminded myself, gripping the carrying case of my laptop. Imagine, I'm researching my dissertation at one of the greatest centers of scholarship in the world. The gnawing doubt that crept into my mind was, What on earth am *I* doing here?

My foray into London's illustrious library was part of a summer of dissertation research funded by a fellowship. I had given my obscure studies the title "British Images of the American West, 1870–1914." Secretly I couldn't help but think how ludicrous it was that someone had actually given me money to work on such a nontopic. But as I spent the summer wandering the halls of the austere British Library, wondering why I was there, my research began to blossom. I started to see the connections between Victorian women travelers in hoopskirts, Sioux warriors, aristocratic ranchers, and potboiling novelists. My topic began to seem real to me, and so I began to believe I could make it seem real to someone else. I believed I had something to say. And maybe, just maybe, I did belong here.

The exultation of watching your intellectual powers flourish alternates with doubt, anxiety, and loneliness during the years it takes to earn your Ph.D. The questions ricochet inside: Am I really smart enough to do this? Will I ever finish? When do I get on with my life? What's the point of reading these arcane books, anyway? At its best, graduate study offers a chance for meaningful intellectual growth. At its worst, it requires you to draw on every ounce of commitment, discipline, and determination you have.

THE JOURNEY BACK

I didn't go directly to graduate school after college. Instead I worked for a year at a variety of jobs. After an endless stream of pending papers and looming exams, it was a joy to no longer have my evenings and weekends tainted by that nagging sense that I should be studying. But as time went by, I found I truly missed the intellectual excitement of the academic world. I felt the working world lacked the blend of modesty and wisdom I had found in my college professors, and my memory of the passion they brought to their work ultimately led me to abandon the rigid nine-to-five schedule to return to school. Three years later, I'm still inspired by the people around me. Perhaps more important, I've also begun to acquire a confidence in my own intellectual abilities.

MORE OF THE SAME?

Earning your Ph.D. is nothing like going to college. What makes it so different? In one sentence: Studying is your job. In graduate school professors expect you to take your work seriously, in the same way that partners at law firms or vice presidents at ad agencies expect the same of their entry-level associates and executives. Academic study is now your career. All of a sudden, it's your responsibility to be an assertive and organized professional. For me, that was a challenge. In college I was never one to seek out professors after class—I wrote strong papers, performed well on exams, and waited to be noticed and rewarded. While it worked fine then, I discovered that in graduate school you can't sit around waiting to be praised. Here you need to knock on doors, voice your opinions, and establish strong relationships with professors. As in any other occupation, personal contacts matter in academia. I'd naively thought that this path offered an escape from the networking and sycophancy that repelled me from other occupations. It was an illusion I quickly had to abandon.

However, successful academic careers are not built on the support of powerful professors alone (at least not usually). They also require premeditated action—the kind of forethought that I eschewed as unnecessary during my undergraduate years. Back then, I rarely planned ahead more than one semester. In graduate school, however, you're supposed to think long-term and take responsibility for your future from the day you arrive. Although you're not expected to have a dissertation topic in hand when you begin, you will need to have come up with one within two or three years. That means taking care of a multitude of preparatory steps. Seeking funding, identifying critical resources, and tracking down experts is all part of your job description as an incoming academic, and failure to fulfill these obligations may leave you clutching for a topic, taking years to finish, or, even worse, hastily writing up a topic you don't care about.

But this preparation is really only the back-burner project. Consuming course work takes precedence during your first few years. Although people's experiences vary depending on their field of study, most Ph.D. students I know acknowledge that they never worked as hard in college as they do now. Taking two seminars a semester, I routinely read through a thousand pages of assigned reading every week, not to mention the journals, articles, and books I'm also expected to keep up on, assigned or not. I have to manage my time and set priorities now in a way I never had to in college. While friends and distractions are necessary to prevent you from becoming a reclusive freak, in graduate school you will probably find yourself tossing Frisbees less than you'd like and hitting the books more than you'd care to.

CAREER STUDENT OR PROFESSIONAL-IN-TRAINING?

Obviously, graduate school deviates from a conventional career in many ways. You don't have to be at the office at nine and you can still wear that disheveled sweater you've had since freshman year. But there's also no fat paycheck deposited in your bank account every two weeks. Fundamentally, you're in a weird intermediate zone between professional definitions while working on your Ph.D. You're not just a college student, but you're not an accredited academic yet. For humanities students, there is usually a six- or seven-year gap between the moment you enter your first graduate seminar and the day you leave your adviser's office with accepted dissertation in hand. The length of that apprenticeship, with its feelings of endlessly delayed gratification, can be one of the most frustrating aspects of grad school. Well-meaning relatives ask you, "So when do you finish?" and you have the perverse fun of shocking them with a truthful estimate. Once in a while, as I watch friends settling into careers and families, I can't escape feeling that I'm wasting the best years of my life.

What keeps me going? Taking a deep breath is a good start, abandoning my library carrel for a walk in the sun helps, and taking a moment to look at the larger picture is essential. As in any other walk of life, one day can seem a lot like the next in graduate school, so it's been important for me to take time now and then to reflect on why I'm here.

Teaching

Fortunately, hiding away in the rafters of academic libraries is not the only responsibility of graduate school. In addition to playing the role of scholar, most graduate students also have the opportunity to become a teacher, or at least a teaching assistant. This is an invaluable way to practice lecturing, guiding discussion, and creating assignments. It also helps an academic connect professionally with the nonacademic world. It can be stressful explaining Rousseau's concept of general will and then looking at a room of puzzled faces, but it can also be fulfilling. As a historian, I find it both challenging and rewarding to make my subject accessible. Rather than try to cram facts and dates down people's throats, I strive to have my students reflect on the differences between past societies and our own. A discussion about the Industrial Revolution can be a forum to discuss the way the economy directly affects our lives. A short document written by a woman during the French Revolution can provoke heated discussions about gender relations and political equality. I don't want to fool myself with grandiose notions about the tremendous impact I have on people's lives, but I do hope I've contributed in some way to their intellectual growth. At the same time, they're helping me. Teaching forces me to sort out what really matters about history from the merely antiquarian.

Joining the Academic Ranks

The academic conversations carried on in journals, at conferences, in seminars, and over beer have their absurd and petty turns, but they can also be deeply exciting. Every day, I'm presented with new ideas and challenged to refine my own. In graduate school I'm in a world where ideas matter. That world contains many dedicated and brilliant people and an opportunity to diversify your surroundings. Depending on your field, you may find yourself traveling the world to find sources for your research, organizing conferences and publications, or working part time in industry, government, or the community. The longer I've been in my Ph.D. program, the more I've come to realize that it's not so much the individual debate or class session that's significant as much as it is the ongoing conversation among scholars. That discussion animates and humanizes; it disturbs and inspires. The knowledge it represents, and the fact that I'm a part of it in some small way, makes even the most frustrating days seem worthwhile.

Some Advice from Monica

Picking a Program: In choosing a college, school reputation means a lot. In choosing a Ph.D. program, it means almost nothing. What does matter is the reputation of the program you're interested in and, perhaps most important, who you can find to be your adviser. In the academic world, having the right faculty member to provide support, guidance, and inspiration makes all the difference. Ultimately this person has a tremendous influence on your success in graduate school and even your life after you complete your degree.

Looking for an Adviser: One of the best sources for help in seeking out programs and potential advisers is your undergraduate professors. Reading journals, academic book publishers' catalogs, and academic texts can also give you leads on professors who are working on subjects that you find interesting.

Applying: If you can, get a graduate student in your field to look over a rough draft of your statement of purpose before you turn in your application. Students who are already in such programs generally have a pretty good sense of what admissions boards are looking for.

Paying for School: Don't give up on going to grad school because you have no money. Although there is little funding for master's programs, most Ph.D. candidates are able to have a substantial portion of their costs paid for them. There is more fellowship support available than you might think (see resources listed below). Many departments also provide their students with teaching assistantships or research assistantships.

A Few Resources to Help You Out

Getting What You Came For: The Smart Student's Guide to Earning a Master's or a Ph.D., by Robert L. Peters (New York: Noonday Press/Farrar, Straus, and Giroux, 1992). What is graduate school really like? Do you need to go? Should you work first? How do you choose a school? How do you improve your credentials for admission? What are your prospects for financial aid? How do you manage your time in grad school? Do you have to play politics? How do you survive qualifying exams? It's all in this book.

Graduate Scholarship Directory: The Complete Guide to Scholarships, Fellowships, Grants and Loans for Graduate and Professional Study, by Daniel J. Cassidy (Hawthorne, N.J.: Career Press, 1995). Lists more than sixteen hundred funding possibilities, indexed both by field of study and by eligibility requirements.

For other resources, see "Getting a Master's Degree," page 165.

TRAVELING

After sixteen years of study you're about to get that degree and plunge into the real world. Now it's time to buckle down and look for a serious job. Or is it?

The window of time after graduation, for most, is a period of few commitments and constraints. You're no longer burdened by classes, papers, and exams, but you haven't yet been tied down to the nine-to-five schedule of a job. This can be the perfect opportunity to both challenge and indulge yourself by taking some time to travel.

Before you move on to the next step in your life, why not spend a year teaching English in Eastern Europe; backpacking through southeast Asia; working at a resort in the Virgin Islands; traveling around the globe on a round-the-world ticket; or living out whatever other travel dream you may have?

The essays in this section describe a few travel adventures by recent graduates. For some graduates, traveling is a chance to get perspective on where they are headed in life. For others, it is a source of renewed self-confidence. For many, it is a way to learn not only about the world, but also more about themselves. It's a life choice that few regret.

Many seniors who entertain the thought of travel, however, have concerns. Most often the question on their mind is "What do graduate schools and potential employers think about students who take time out to travel after college?"

The truth is, admissions officers and employers can be very

supportive of traveling. A person who has taken the initiative to embark on his or her own postgraduate adventure is looked upon as someone who is willing to challenge him- or herself.

"We look favorably on applicants who have done something interesting or unique after undergraduate work," says one member of the UCLA graduate admissions board. "Traveling can only add to someone's experience."

A potential employer who knows you've taken the initiative to travel on your own may think of you as motivated and independent. At the very least, it will give you something interesting to discuss in an interview.

Many grads who take time to travel also find that it's a great way to evaluate their goals and then reconfirm their commitments. Or, if you're like most college seniors and have no idea what's next, traveling can be a chance to take a step back, think about your life, and come back to the States more focused.

It's true traveling after college is not the right choice for everyone. You may be anxious to plunge right into grad school or a career you know is right for you, and if you have that passion, more power to you. But if you don't have that focused drive, or even if you do and simply want to take a break, traveling is worth considering. As one graduate bitten by the wanderlust bug put it, "You've got forty more years to pursue your career, but how many times in your life can you buy a one-way ticket, throw some clothes into a backpack, and set out to see the world?"

Working Your
Way Through
Europe

Kirsten Lee Soares

Many grads rule out travel after college because they don't have any money, but Kirsten's tale proves that such an obstacle can be overcome. In this essay she describes some of the adventures she had working her way through Europe.

If you long for whimsical towns and open roads, follow your wanderlust. Do it. Do it before some big corporation swallows your spirit.

Even if you're constrained by low funds, you can work your way in and out of almost any country. Most guidebooks advise that to work in Europe, you must be a resident of the European Community or a student holding an International Student Identification Card. I was neither. Finding work to pay for your travels is simply a matter of diligence and timing.

After graduation, I certainly didn't have the ideal baggage: I had monthly student loans, a debt owed on my Volkswagen bug, and only $1,000 saved from a year of working after college. I also did not have parents who could fund my foray abroad. But the more time I spent after graduation working under fluorescent office lights, the more itchy I grew for an adventure. I decided that if I couldn't afford a pure vacation experience, I'd seek out odd jobs abroad that would throw me into random towns and cities, allowing me to work with different people and then move on.

KNOCKING ON DOORS

Job hunting as a traveler is about knocking on doors. It's a matter of persistence and ingenuity, watching for every opportunity and seizing whatever comes your way. I discovered this when, after buying a cheap one-way ticket to Europe, I found myself on the streets of Galway, Ireland, with a backpack, a quickly diminishing stack of traveler's checks in my waist pouch, and no friends or contacts around. Having squandered half of my trip's funds exploring the theaters and pubs of Dublin and Belfast, I had to start looking for work.

I targeted hotels first because I knew I could save more money for travel if my room and board were provided. That first day I optimistically inquired at fifteen of the town's top establishments— the biggest hotels, bed and breakfast inns, and hostels. No job. The following day I lowered my standards to restaurants. Then I slipped down to inquiring at the little boutiques and pottery shops, willing to take any kind of work they could offer. Everyone's answer was the same: it was nearly the end of July and their staffs were complete.

The next day was Saturday, and though I preferred the charm of Galway, I decided I'd have to head back to Dublin to look for work in a bigger city. En route to the train station, I found myself fighting my way through throngs of people, all dressed unusually well—women in gloves and big flowered hats, men in suits with little knit vests. A sidewalk accordion player told me these tourists were in town for the horse races, and I immediately doubled back. Someone was going to have to pamper those tourists and it might as well be me. With renewed optimism, I took another crack at the hotels and within an hour found a proprietor who admitted that his dining room was ill prepared for the holiday and could use another pair of hands. At last, after surviving three fifteen-hour

days waitressing during the horse-racing rush, I was hired on full time.

Admittedly, the job was not glamorous. I spent the next month changing dirty sheets, scrubbing toilets, and pulling wads of hair out of shower drains. But I was living in Ireland, a block away from the coastline where the Galway Bay yawns out to meet the Aran Islands. And while I toiled during the day to refill my depleted money pouch, the nights were mine to enjoy Irish drinking and dancing, tipping the fiddlers and harpists along the way. After four weeks I had made another $800 to spend exploring the ice caves of the Swiss Alps and enjoying a cornucopia of food and drink in the cafés along the Seine.

SPREADING THE WORD

Uncovering job leads while traveling is also about broadcasting your needs. Success is often simply a matter of letting everyone you meet know you're looking for work: the guy at the hostel's front desk, the guy behind the bar, other backpackers, and anyone else you might run into. I have also met people who have found jobs by putting up signs on bulletin boards in train stations, launderettes, and tourist information bureaus. When you need work, it pays to not be bashful.

Before I'd left the States, I had heard romantic stories about people who'd made their way across the European continent picking grapes. The only problem was I wasn't sure where to find a landowner who would hire a woman whose work experiences were in the offices of urban America and not in the fields. Then one night, while drinking with the hotel's night watchman, I learned that he had a friend who had a friend who owned property in France's Beaujolais Valley. He shared the address with me.

After several weeks of pure travel in France and Switzerland, I found myself in the grape vineyards north of Lyon, watching the sun rise over a tangle of greens in the morning, laboring as a migrant worker during the day, drinking wine in the fields, and eating like a lord when the day's labor was done.

The accommodations were simple. There were about thirty of us—French students, Polish families, Norwegian women, the Irish, and a handful of Americans—all shacked up in an old barn with rusted beds. We shared one shower and one Turkish toilet, a glorified hole in the ground covered in plastic.

We spent our days hunched over the vines, slashing away at the grapes with our sickle knives. We were dirty, our backs ached, our hands were swollen and cut. I have never been so content.

In the fields we passed the time sharing stories about our different worlds. At night we holed up in our rural barracks and picked guitars and debated politics. Through it all, the landowners treated us to lavish homemade meals.

At dawn the farmers' wives would wake us with steamed milk and warm French bread. After an hour in the fields, the owner would open up the back of his truck and we took our breaks with chocolates and cheese, fresh salami, and two pitchers of liquid. Always two. One poured water and one poured wine, and the

French workers tapped the purple liquor like a thirst quencher, no matter the hour. They drank it beginning at nine in the morning until the sun sank and then straight on through the night.

And then there was dinner. After working in the fields all day, we'd come in exhausted but in high spirits, anticipating the meal that awaited us. It was a smorgasbord of international toasts, conversations in four different languages, the Poles boasting *"Nastrovya,"* the French *"Cin Cin,"* a Gaelic greeting, the English "Cheers," and our Australian friend unabashedly shouting, "Get it in 'ya." Green beans in a vinaigrette followed roast beef. Brie followed salad. Pastries followed fruit and wine and more wine. The owners would emerge from the cellars with the product of our labor, proudly placing bottle after bottle on the table. We feasted like guests rather than laborers.

Living on a farm was ideal for the working traveler because our routine left no time for squandering away the money we earned. Every day I spent working in those fields, my travel funds grew by about $40. It was difficult work. I was dirty. I was sweaty. It was also the highlight of my whole trip. The simple things in life—a hot shower, good food, and good conversation—became my biggest pleasures. And when I walked away from the farm, I had another $600 stashed away.

As I continued to ride the rackety rails of Europe, I met more and more people working their way across the Continent, always willing to trade clothes, books, and cassettes or swap advice about where there was work. One traveler was following the various harvests—tomatoes in Italy, olives in Greece, walnuts in Germany. A couple from New Zealand had been working in the London pubs on and off for three years, working only until they had enough cash to take off for the savannahs of Africa or the pyramids of Egypt, returning to England only when their funds ran low. Another traveler earned his keep by riding a bicycle up and down the hazardous London streets, delivering sandwiches to zealous businessmen. Each new working traveler's tale reaffirmed what I was finding out for myself: if you're willing to be creative, you can pay for your travels. If you can bus tables, hammer a nail, pluck an apple, or change a diaper, you won't starve, and by paying for your passage, you may find your adventures that much more fulfilling.

Ultimately, having to work to finance my time overseas made my time more meaningful than a holiday could have ever been. When I finished hitchhiking those narrow, small-town roads, navigating my way in and out of countries where I could not speak in English, uncovering work, food, and shelter, I had a new sense of strength and completeness.

If you have similar desires, chase them. Throw caution to the wind and go.

Some Advice from Kirsten

Starting Money: By sleeping in pensions and hostels and enjoying bread and wine along the Seine, you can tour Europe on about $40 to $50 a day. I started out with a Eurail pass and $1,000. That sum seems laughable now, but at the time, I was determined to go. Figure out what standard of living you want to maintain and plan accordingly.

When to Get Work: Give yourself a financial buffer. I told myself that whenever I was down to $500, I'd look for work. With a buffer you can be more choosy and less frantic while you look for work.

Looking for Work: Have an idea about what kinds of work you could tolerate. Do you prefer nude modeling in art studios to watching spoiled toddlers? Would you rather tend bar or bang nails? One woman I met traveled with her cookbooks, hoping to do prep work in the kitchens of yachts sailing the Mediterranean.

A good place to start your search is the youth hostels. Staff members generally speak English and many times they can use you on staff to cook or clean in exchange for room and board and a small stipend. Bulletin boards in English-speaking bookstores, launderettes, and train stations can also offer ideas.

Working the Farm Circuit: Some backpackers have found that they can move from one harvest season to the next. Once you latch on to one job, it's easy to jump to the next one. If you try to go the official route, you will have a tougher time, since without dual citizenship, you cannot work without being a member of the EC. I suggest just showing up. In the middle of the harvest season it is unlikely that a landowner would turn down an extra body. (For information on harvest seasons in Europe, pick up *Work Your Way Around the World*, by Susan Griffith—see below).

Traveling Alone: When you travel alone, you always choose the direction when the road forks. Away from the constant company of another American, you will be more likely to forge ahead, making friends with travelers young and old from around the world. And the solitude, especially on the trains, offers time for reflection and decision making.

Safety: You just have to be aware of your surroundings—really nothing more than the common sense you apply in the States. When I was traveling, I'd think twice about going out after dark. But to be honest, I didn't feel I needed to be any more aware than I need to be here. In a lot of respects I feel less safe in a city here in the States than I did when I was traveling.

A Few Resources to Help You Out

Air Hitch ([212] 864-2000). A low-budget, self-help travel service primarily for recent graduates and students. If you are flexible, Air Hitch can get you to Europe cheap by putting you on underbooked commercial flights. It also flies to the Caribbean and selected U.S. cities.

Council on International Education Exchange (205 East Forty-second Street, New York, N.Y. 10017, [212] 661-1414). CIEE, an extremely valuable organization, is committed to helping people interested in international travel and education. One of its best services is a work-abroad program for students and recent graduates that may include a legal work permit for Great Britain, Ireland, France, West Germany, New Zealand, or Costa Rica. CIEE also offers a variety of travel services: discount airline tickets, charter flights, student discount cards, and travel guides.

Work, Study, Travel Abroad: The Whole World Handbook, ed. Del Franz and Lararo Hernandez and the Council on International Educational

Exchange (New York: St. Martin's Press, 1995). An excellent country-by-country guide that provides travel advice and resources for recent graduates interested in working abroad, studying abroad, or simply traveling on a budget.

Work Your Way Around the World, by Susan Griffith (Oxford: Vacation Work, 1983; distributed in the United States by Writer's Digest Books, Cincinnati). Filled with job ideas—advice on how to get work on private yachts or commercial ships, listings of the harvest seasons in Europe, organizations to contact to be an air courier, listings of companies that need people to deliver cars in Africa, suggestions for working on a kibbutz in Israel, and plenty more. The only drawback is that it's a British publication. At times this can be frustrating, since some of the jobs require European citizenship. Still, there are more than enough opportunities for Americans to make the book well worth purchasing.

How to Get a Job in Europe, by Robert Sanborn (Chicago: Surrey Books, 1995). Offers information on both permanent and temporary employment. It contains country-by-country profiles listing American companies and outlining employment regulations for Americans. It also includes listings of volunteer opportunities, international nonprofit organizations, hotel employers, and teaching organizations.

Directory of Overseas Summer Jobs, by David Woodworth (Princeton, N.J.: Peterson's Guides, 1995). Everything from being an au pair in Austria to picking strawberries in France to being a sailing instructor in Greece is in this book. Particularly useful to travelers with work permits through the CIEE work-study program.

Teaching

English

in Eastern

Europe

Roger Bearden

Beneath the soot-filled skies and towering spires of Eastern Europe there is a burgeoning population of American expatriates who've come to live in this intriguing and rapidly changing part of the world. After college, Roger chose to spend a year in the Czech and Slovack Republics. Here are his thoughts on this memorable experience.

Teaching English in Eastern Europe offers an array of fulfilling experiences. Eating Eastern European food offers . . . well, *halushki*.

A month out of college, I discovered both of these lessons upon moving to Nitra, a small town in Slovakia. I stayed with a host family that took great pride in offering me their national dish, *halushki*. It was a tasty meal—small potato shells layered with cream, bacon, and cheese—and I enjoyed my first sampling thoroughly. The next night, however, several of my students took me out to a restaurant. "Try our national dish," they told me and ordered some *halushki*. The following night, at a student's house, dinner was served. *"Halushki?"* I said with feigned curiosity. For two more nights, gracious hosts served me *halushki*, and each time

I exclaimed with delight at the newfound discovery. On the sixth night, I went out for pizza.

Choosing to live and work in this undeveloped but rapidly evolving part of the world can be both a humorous and rewarding educational experience. The food can be mundane, the phone system frustrating, and the bureaucracy mind numbing, but the people and culture have much to offer. And as I can attest from personal experience, teaching in a foreign country is never dull.

VELVET REVOLUTION

The changes that swept through Eastern Europe during the late eighties and early nineties opened new passages for young travelers. I was one of the many young Americans eager to explore. I fell in love with Central Europe during a month I spent in Prague during college and decided to return after graduation to teach English. Living in a country that had essentially dispensed with vowels appealed to me. A strange wish, I know, but I figured that any language that used words like *smrt* and *prst* ("death" and "finger," respectively) was something worth investigating.

LIFE IN THE LAND OF BUREAUCRACY

Unfortunately, vowels are not the only thing missing in Eastern Europe. If you've heard tales about these countries being mired in bureaucracy and lacking basic services we take for granted, I assure you, they are all true. Take the phones, for example. Try using a residential phone during the day and your Czech friends will laugh at you. As my host family explained after my fifth attempt to call my employer upon arrival, business phones have priority during business hours. Jiri, my host, gave it to me straight: it's easier to take the metro to an office than to try to call it.

As for bureaucracies, being a teacher in Eastern Europe, at times, can be like running in a maze. A few months in the Czech Republic will give you a far better understanding of Kafka than any senior literature seminar could ever hope. There is a labyrinth of rules governing foreign workers that would confound even the greatest of bureaucrats. You must have an official work permit, without which you cannot sign a work contract or be paid. Of course, you can't receive a work permit until you've signed a work contract. Like many regulations here, it's a classic catch-22 that requires you to break the law somewhere along the way before you accomplish anything.

There's also the medical system. In the Czech Republic, your doctor is determined by your address. My street address, Heyrovskeho 31, meant I could see the doctor behind door 41 in clinic 3. I could do this, however, only during office hours, which were from 7:00 A.M. to 10:30 A.M. on a first-come, first-served basis. The day I went to see a doctor about bronchitis, I arrived at six to stand in line. I wasn't seen until nine. The examination itself took five minutes and the next twenty were spent waiting while an office worker typed up a bewildering variety of forms. In the end I found it simpler to buy myself something at the pharmacy.

ENGLISH 101

Of course, no one goes to Eastern Europe for the sole purpose of being subjected to such bureaucratic mishaps. A more rewarding element of the experience for many is the opportunity to teach English. Although the increasing number of foreigners is making it more difficult, many travelers who come here find teaching positions at private language schools, businesses, or public schools.

In my case, I was hired for the academic year as an English conversation teacher in a Czech public high school. When I took the position, I naively thought my work would be coordinated with that of other English teachers in the school. What I found was that the school supplied me with a list of topics that my twelve classes of twenty students might find interesting. The only other direction I was given was that conversation lessons were to last two hours. Everything else was up to me.

Left to my own devices, I decided that my goal as a teacher was to give my students room to develop their English through role play and discussion and to let them guide the course of their study according to their interests. I consciously wanted to subvert the Czech idea that a student learns (that is, memorizes) and a teacher teaches (tells the students the facts to memorize). My classroom, I hoped, would be a noisy, loosely structured place for students to learn.

It didn't exactly start out that way. When I walked into my classroom for the first time, the students stood, facing forward toward the blackboard. I proceeded to the front of the room and put my books down. I smiled, wrote my name on the board, and introduced myself. Eerily, my students continued to stand. I looked at them inquiringly. I told them where I was from and that I was the new English conversation teacher. They continued to stand. If it hadn't been for a student in the front row who whispered that I was supposed to tell them to sit down, who knows how long this standoff would have lasted. Every class, it turned out, began with the students standing as a sign of respect to the teacher.

As time went on, my students and I loosened up and learned together. Being around young people, whose personal development mirrored the free Czech society at large, was intoxicating. With English being a gateway to business, travel, literature, and ideas, they were hungry to learn. Jana, a fiery fifteen-year-old, wanted to learn English so that she could become a lawyer and emigrate to the United States to help Native Americans get their land back. Petr wanted to understand Schwarzenegger movies. Jan, who built cameras and model planes from scrap parts, wanted to understand English technical manuals. Another Jan, whose abundant brown curls and wire-rimmed glasses made him a dead ringer for John Lennon, had learned his English from Doors albums and Shakespeare's sonnets. He yearned to master English poetry.

As with any experience abroad, developing friendships with these people and learning about their culture helped to make my time fulfilling. My students showed me the joys of going "on the wander," the Czech tradition of hiking around the countryside and making rest stops at the local pubs. They also taught me the polka

and laughed while I made a mockery of myself during the professors' dance at the school ball.

Welcome to Amerika

The Czechs have a funny reverence for American culture. Pizen, the town where I spent much of my time, has changed what was once Moscow Street to America Street. Residents can shop at Kmart and eat at McDonald's. Along the same byway, you'll now find the American Fast Food Sport Bar filled with Czechs wearing varsity jackets for sports teams that don't exist. (My personal favorite was "Detroit Rednecks.") Sadly, teachers may one day come to Eastern Europe to find an environment resembling the one they left behind. But for now Eastern Europe is still an incredible place to spend some time after college.

I didn't return from my time teaching abroad with a lot of money.

Americans don't get rich in Eastern Europe. In fact, few break even. But I did take home a working knowledge of a language with no vowels, memories of many good people I'd met along the way, and a desire never to eat *halushki* again.

Some Advice from Roger

Finding a Job: There are a number of American nonprofit organizations that bring teachers to Eastern Europe (see resources below). Private language schools will often hire teachers on the spot, though the reputable ones will look for previous experience or a teaching degree.

Learning the Language: I'd advise anyone going to an Eastern European country to try to pick up some of the language before they leave or to take a language course once they arrive. The people I know who did this found themselves more satisfied with their overall teaching experience.

Teaching Materials: Bring as many resources as your suitcase will allow. Many schools have only a set of basic textbooks and will expect you to bring your own materials. Also, the British Council, an arm of the British government, has set up a number of English Teaching Resource Centers throughout Eastern Europe to provide materials for teachers and students of English. I found them invaluable.

Health: Pollution is a huge problem in Eastern Europe. Much of the region's energy comes from the burning of coal, and most cars lack smog control. Those with lung problems should think seriously before going to Eastern Europe. Also, outside of the major cities, fresh vegetables are hard to come by during the winter. Learn to love the potato.

A Few Resources to Help You Out

Teaching English Abroad, by Susan Griffith (Oxford: Vacation Work, 1994; distributed in the United States by Peterson's Guides, Princeton, N.J.). A valuable source for general teaching advice and resources, including a list of English schools to contact abroad. Divided by country, each chapter has suggestions on how to find jobs, a description of working conditions, and listings of state schools, private schools, and volunteer organizations.

World Teach (Harvard Institute for International Development, One Elliot Street, Cambridge, Mass. 02138, [617] 495-5527). A program designed for young adults who wish to be volunteer English teachers in developing nations. It offers year-long programs in Costa Rica, Ecuador, Namibia, Thailand, Poland, South Africa, and Russia.

Georgetown University Internship Program (P.O. Box 2298, Hoya Station, Washington, D.C. 20057, [202] 298-0200). A program that recruits college graduates to teach English overseas. It sponsors programs in Poland, Czechoslovakia, Bulgaria, China, Egypt, Russia, Belarus, Latvia, and the Ukraine. Fees start at $1,500.

Czech Academic Information Agency (c/o Dum Zahranichich Styku, Senovazne Namesti 26, 11121 Prague, Czech Republic). A volunteer teaching program. Candidates are screened in the United States.

Education for Democracy (USA) Ltd. (P.O. Box 40514, Mobile, Ala. 36640-0514, [205] 434-3889). This organization places self-financing English as a Second Language (ESL) teachers in the Czech or Slovak Republic for a minimum of five months.

Mountain

Biking

Through Latin

America

Steve de Brun

This essay is as much about finding a way to travel as it is about traveling itself. On the following pages, Steve writes about how a crazy idea conceived on a New York subway was transformed into a realistic plan and ultimately an unforgettable journey through the towns and trails of Latin America.

Six months after graduating from college, a friend and I mounted bicycles in Los Angeles and rode south through the Americas to Santiago, Chile. Our journey spanned eleven months and twelve countries. It took us across three time zones and through numerous cultures. Along the way it allowed us to take an idea and turn it into an expedition.

During my senior year in college, I wasn't exactly excited about doing the job interview thing. Drawing up a résumé of my "accomplishments," scanning the job listings, and scrambling for interview slots wasn't really for me. To be honest, I was a little intimidated by classmates who had focused career goals and concrete plans to attain them. I did know, however, what I liked to do for fun. I enjoyed speaking Spanish and spending time outside. It's not surprising that these two passions became the topic of discussion one winter day on a New York subway. While my classmates were developing practical plans for the future, I found myself on the N train fantasizing with a friend about hopping on a bike, attaching a surfboard to the back, and exploring the coasts of the Americas.

Living out *Endless Summer* on two wheels wasn't a practical idea, but once it was planted in my head, it was hard to let it go. As I sloshed through the snow of New England, I couldn't shake this vision of cycling through a tropical village somewhere thousands of miles to the south. During the next few months, I kept sharing the idea with friends and family. The more I talked about it, the more I started to believe in it. By summer I had a committed travel partner and a revised plan: we would pedal south from California, write a newsletter to document and pay for our journey, and raise a little money for a good cause or two along the way.

How We Did It—Starting from Scratch

Our research for this trip was haphazard and directed mostly by the suggestions of other people. Essentially my travel partner and I told everyone we knew that we were planning to bicycle from California to Chile and asked for ideas on how we could pull this off. Not everyone was helpful. Some acquaintances would give us that dumbfounded why-would-you-do-that? look, usually accompanied by "How about backpacking through Europe?" But most people had a good suggestion or two. Through this word-of-mouth research, we discovered the South American Explorer's Club, which helped us plot our route. Friends also led us to the third world studies department of my school, where we learned about the nonprofit organizations that worked to benefit Latin America.

During this time I would also go to the library, open an atlas to a spread of the western hemisphere, and drool. Today I still love to do this, but now I reminisce over the roadside stops, vicious mountain ranges, and amazing people we met along the way.

Forming a Nonprofit

After talking, reading, and brainstorming, our plan began to crystallize. We decided to leave the surfboards at home, create a small not-for-profit company called Bicycling for Awareness and Responsible Development (BARD), and raise money for two already-established nonprofits. We chose the nonprofits based on their aid philosophies and their willingness and enthusiasm to work with us. To promote our adventure, we made a small pamphlet that described who we were and for whom we were raising money. On the back cover, we also mentioned we were selling a newsletter to document our passage south and we sold subscriptions to it at various price levels. The most basic subscription purchased a newsletter, gave a small sum to the nonprofits, and contributed to our trip expenses. As the price went up, so did the benefits of membership: we offered T-shirts to the higher-level subscribers.

It was important that our pamphlet look professional but not too slick, otherwise people might think we already had substantial funding. So I designed it myself. I also gratefully accepted some layout assistance from a graphic artist friend, whose time was paid for by another graphic artist friend as her donation to our effort. Here I was introduced to the concept of the "in-kind donation." Numerous friends and companies helped our cause by donating other equipment or services pertinent to the trip. A local print shop cut us a good deal to print, collate, and staple the pamphlets. Collateral in hand, we set out to spread the good word.

Finding Support

We began the mechanics-in-motion phase by sending pamphlets to everyone we knew. Then we showered news organizations, equipment manufacturers, and other companies with letters, press releases, and pamphlets. Little by little, we started to see results: An athletic wear company gave us Gore-Tex rain suits. A camping gear manufacturer offered sleeping pads. A small fine-art reproduction company in Con-

HI! I'M FROM B.Y.K.R., A SMALL AMERICAN NON-PROFIT. PERHAPS YOU'D LIKE SOME OF OUR LITERATURE.

necticut gave us free posters, which we were able to sell at universities and colleges in the Northeast. Local papers picked up our press releases and gave us a call. Best of all, a bike manufacturer gave us new bicycles, two of last year's models that were being replaced by new inventory.

During this period, we both worked various odd jobs and saved as much money as possible. This was ramen noodles and peanut butter and jelly time. To cut expenses, I also moved in with my parents the last four months before our departure. Every dollar we saved we pumped into the trip fund.

Concurrent with our marketing and publicity efforts, we prepared, as much as we could, emotionally, intellectually, and physically for the journey. There is no substitute workout for riding a bike eight hours a day, and inevitably, the first month of riding was full of metabolic crashes and intimidating hills.

Finally our departure day arrived. We were eager to turn our abstract idea into something real. Talk is talk, but we didn't really know if we could pull this trip off.

TAKING OFF

We said good-bye to the people we loved and pedaled out of Santa Monica on a crisp winter morning. It didn't take us long to realize that our legs were too inexperienced to push those overloaded bikes down the California coast, and we started to get rid of anything weighing us down. We sent home anything large, heavy, and not absolutely necessary; then small, dense things; then large, light things.

Slowly, though, we developed a rhythm. Our daily routine revolved around simple activities. We cherished sleep as a time of peace and physical regeneration. We ate constantly, because food powered our two-leg motors. Reading and writing were valuable ways to pass the time in the shade and record memories, revelations, and communications. Meeting people and crossing the many ensuing cultural and linguistic bridges occupied much of our time, especially in cities. And, of course, we rode. My rear hurt nonstop the first two weeks. It felt like Chinese water torture, except my butt was my head and my bike was the drop of water. We learned, from trial and error, which foods fueled our bodies most efficiently, what kinds of stretches were good for biking, what cadence was sustainable for hours on end, and how far we could reasonably go before we would exhaust ourselves.

Along the way we had our adventures. In Panama City we managed to talk ourselves onto an air force base in the Canal Zone. We had heard there was a motorcycle club sympathetic to cyclists on this base, so we called the sponsor and he let us sleep in a grimy but acceptable garage for a week while we were waiting for a ship to go south. We spent our days exploring the city and perusing biker magazines, while we laid in bed at night drenched with sweat. During our stay we met people like Boaz, a crazy Israeli motorcyclist who had stopped in Mexico to learn the craft of guitar making and traveled with his own hand-made instrument hanging out of his panniers.

In Ecuador we found an Amazonian jungle lodge whose owner let us work for room and board and gave us the opportunity to spend some time in the mature-growth tropical rain forest. We descended to the jungle and for two weeks lugged sand on sleds through the steamy vegetation, then into a canoe, and through the jungle once again to the future site of a water tower. We learned to paddle a canoe and speak a little of the indigenous tongue, Quechua. We were also taught how to balance long bamboo trunks, kerosene, potatoes, fruits, and planks on our shoulders. As we trudged through the jungle each day, we learned the many calls of the brilliantly colored birds, peered at monkeys, gawked at outrageous bugs, and tested the medicinal plants under the watchful eye of knowledgeable guides. To top it off, we even tasted live ants.

As our journey progressed, we also found out more about ourselves. We began to question our "hard-guy" attitude. Many people who tour long distances on bicycles tend to experience this hard-guy phenomenon—a compulsion to prove to yourself that you can achieve great distances, with considerable hardship and asceticism. As we continued southward, we chose to pedal less and enjoy life a little more.

At various points during the trip, friends and family joined us for a visit or to ride. How truly bizarre and wonderful it is to meet a good friend in a foreign land and explore it by bicycle. Luckily, we met up with our friends after our hard-guy stage, so they weren't subjected to that nonsense.

To share our trip with our sponsors, we tried to put our tales into words. We wrote newsletters on air mail paper and sent them back to be produced at world headquarters, aka our parents' basements. Communication back to the States was relatively easy in cities, and when we were in the countryside, we enjoyed our isolation. During our journey, we also met with representatives from the nonprofits for whom we raised money, and visited some community-based grass-roots projects. Our philanthropic efforts were limited once we were on the road, though, and to be honest, most of our time was spent traveling, exploring, and corresponding with home.

Looking back at our letters, I have much to smile at—climbing Mexico's second-highest volcano, being chased by vicious dogs, avoiding various large and biting insects, and plenty of other misadventures. Thanks to this trip, I carry all of these experiences with me now.

Our journey was something that started out as an impractical vision. But through inquiry, philanthropy, and persistence, we were able to turn this dream into an expedition. There is nothing superhuman about what we did. What differentiates us from others is that we actually did it.

Some Advice from Steve

Money: If you live cheap, money goes a long way in Latin America. Every country has a different rate to the dollar, but in general we paid $1 to $3 for meals and $1 to $10 for lodging when were weren't camping. We carried traveler's checks (American Express is widely recognized in the Americas) and occasionally had money wired to us in large cities. We carried no more than $100 cash on our person at any time, so that loss or theft wouldn't be too damaging.

Raising Funds: I found that the most enthusiastic and dedicated support we received was from friends, family, and people to whom we were referred. Cold calls and letters were much less successful. That doesn't mean they're not worth trying; just don't be discouraged if most turn you down.

Communication: If you have an American Express card and a rough idea of your itinerary, you can have friends and family send mail to American Express offices along the way. These offices will hold your mail for you for a while.

Documents: A passport and international health card are mandatory. I carried a birth certificate and photocopies of all documents as well. We also left photocopies at home, so that if anything was lost or stolen, we would at least have the ID numbers of the documents. We also carried documents that showed bike registration in a town or county. This was kind of silly, we thought, but a few unscrupulous border officers actually required documentation of our bike ownership.

Health Insurance: If you can afford it, I'd strongly recommend getting international traveler's insurance. It's fairly expensive (mine was $600 a year) but covers you in case of catastrophic illness. The deductible is high, but what's important is that it will provide immediate care and airlift in a drastic situation.

Local Care: I discovered on this trip that pharmacists double as doctors in much of Latin America. This means that if you have strep, for example, you can go to a pharmacy, tell them you have strep, and they will sell you a bottle of penicillin. No prescription. No paperwork. During our journey I visited local pharmacies for ear infections, viruses, and strep. I am not saying this is necessarily the best way to run things, but it made getting medicine quick and much less expensive.

Water Purification: We used a number of methods: hand-held pump filters, iodine, chlorine, and boiling. If I could do it again, I would get a high-end expedition filter (such as the ones made by Katadyn) that uses ceramic and activated carbon. These are small and effective, and the ceramic filter can be scrubbed clean. They are expensive ($150 to $250), but in the long run I would say they're worth it.

A Few Resources to Help You Out

South American Explorers Club (126 Indian Creek Road, Ithaca, N.Y. 14850, [607] 277-0488). This organization is a rich resource for travel information on Mexico and Central and South America.

The Green Travel Sourcebook: A Guide for the Physically Active, and Intellectually Curious, or the Socially Aware, by Daniel and Sally Wiener Grotta (New York: John Wiley, 1991). Written by a pair of green travelers, this book offers ideas, advice, and resources for travel adventures that take you off the beaten path.

Latin America by Bike: A Complete Touring Guide, by Walter Sienko (Seattle: The Mountaineers, 1993). A well-researched travel guide written specifically for bicycle adventurers. Includes recommended routes, pro- files of regional terrain and road conditions, advice on camping and accommodations, and tips for buying, outfitting, and maintaining your bicycle.

Hostelling-International–American Youth Hostels (Program Department, 733 Fifteenth Street NW, Suite 840, Washington, D.C. 20005, [202] 783-6161. E-mail: Dkalter@ATTMAIL.COM). HI-AYH is more than a place to stay while traveling. This group also puts together low-budget group bicycling trips. Some of its recent tours included a thirty-eight-day excursion down the Pacific Coast from Seattle to San Francisco, an eight-day tour of Scotland's Hebrides Islands, and a three-month trek from Maine to Oregon. Call or write for a brochure of upcoming trips.

Backroads Bicycle Touring (1516 Fifth Street, Berkeley, Calif. 94710, [800] 245-3874). Organizes bicycle trips around the United States and abroad. Adventures range from a weekend in northern California to a multiweek journey through New Zealand.

Outward Bound USA (384 Field Parks Road, Greenwich, Conn. 06800, [800] 243-8570). A nonprofit organization that puts together physically, and often emotionally challenging, outdoor adventures. Programs offered include canoeing, backpacking, mountaineering, sea kayaking, sailing, whitewater rafting, skiing, dog sledding, and winter camping.

Volunteer Vacations: Short-Term Adventures that Will Benefit You and Others, by Bill McMillon (Chicago: Chicago Review Press, 1995). This reference guide provides information on more than 240 organizations that sponsor volunteer projects. Opportunities described include everything from distributing medical supplies in Guatemala to protecting leatherback turtle eggs in the Virgin Islands.

Teaching

English

in Japan

Donna Choo

Who would have thought that something you learned while still in diapers might be one of your most marketable skills after college? Around the world, people are eager to learn English, and in some places, such as Japan, they're even willing to pay you to teach them. In this essay, Donna writes about what she discovered as a teacher in the Japanese government—sponsored Japan Exchange and Teaching (JET) program.

Ask me about my experience in Japan and a haphazard gush of memories come to mind. I feel the cool of oozing mud between my toes while bending to plant rice seedlings. I smell the clean, crisp tatami (straw) mat flooring that covered my entire house. I think of sitting in a natural hot spring bath before a backdrop of white mountains and snow-fringed branches, then coming home to a rich paper house with no central heating and a frozen toilet. I remember a Christmas Day greeting from students huddled on my doorstep laden with presents and food. I recall the cherished solitude an empty bus offered the only *gaijin* (foreigner) in a small rice-farming village where celebrity status was unavoidable.

Through this flood of recollections, I'm amused to think of the path that led me from an American urban college community to a rural Japanese lifestyle. There was no real scheme that motivated my application to the Japanese Exchange and Teaching (JET) program. One day, while waiting for a lunch date, a poster pinned up on a bulletin board simply caught my eye.

As an English major, I had no idea where to take the next step on the ladder to a genuine career or, in fact, which ladder it would be. A year abroad seemed like a good idea—excitement and faraway adventure. This expectation was certainly met. What I didn't bargain for, however, was the dispiriting loneliness and the often deep introspection it inspired. I also didn't expect I would willingly opt for a second year, or that I would actually come to crave the familiar flavor of a McDonald's cheeseburger.

TEACHING OPTIONS

There are several different ways to begin teaching English in Japan. Many graduates line up employment with an established program here in the States before departure, usually with an after-school tutorial school or corporate executive-training program. Other, more spontaneous travelers fly over without a position and hope for the best when they arrive.

The less structured route offers the possibility of uncovering the most lucrative tutoring and teaching positions, along with the flexibility to shape your work schedule to match your lifestyle. It also carries the risk that you'll find yourself in an extremely expensive country without a job. Additionally, without a secure position, should you need help in an emergency or even with the mundane everyday details, no one will be there for you to rely on.

Although I didn't anticipate it, one of the benefits I enjoyed with an established program was its security and the support network it offered. Before I left for Japan, I was deluged with Japanese languages tapes and cultural texts from the Japanese embassy, along with a contract for employment, literature about the area where I was to teach, and photos with a description of my new house. During my two years in Japan, representatives from the Ministry of Education were always available to assist me, from explaining my phone bill to acting as arbitrator and cultural interpreter with my supervisor.

No Experience Required

A typical explanation for why graduates choose to live and work in Japan after college doesn't seem to exist. My colleagues there brought with them diverse backgrounds and divergent interests. They returned to the States to follow equally disparate careers in everything from journalism to environmental studies to economics. I think whether motivated by naïveté or romantic pursuits, most simply leaped.

Fortunately for leapers, few teaching programs expect applicants to have experience. In fact, a lack of Japanese cultural knowledge or language skills is often preferred. Some participants I know went to Japan without ever having eaten with chopsticks. Few had any knowledge of the country whatsoever. Now back in the States, however, many of these same people have maintained an abiding interest in the language and culture of Japan and still crave a good bowl of *ramen* (noodles in hot broth) with *gyoza* (dumplings on the side).

Teaching with JET

Just as those who end up in Japan come for different reasons, the teaching experiences they find are equally diverse. Some areas of the country are more willing than others to accept the inundation of foreign English teachers. Some teachers will value your ideas and treat you as an equal partner. Others will simply ask you to read the textbook and have the class repeat. This is where personal integrity decides what you will gain from the job. In some instances, simply being a native English speaker is enough. You will not be asked to do much more than show up and you will still be paid. Some JET participants do just that. Others decide where they can

make a difference and channel their energy in that direction, participating in after-school sports clubs or starting up exchanges with
schools back home.

When you're teaching in Japan, representing the United States
is also a job. As a resident expert, I was bombarded with constant
questions about America. Once I was asked to give a speech on the
American way of life. Where do you begin? Students came over to
watch television shows my mother had taped and mailed to me.
How do you explain a National Rifle Association commercial?
Each time I opened my mouth to reply to such queries, I could see
in the inquisitive eyes of my audience that they believed my reply
was on behalf of the people of the United States.

Simply being a gaijin in Japan is also an experience. For teachers
near or in a metropolitan area, where foreigners are common, the
commotion associated with the presence of an American is minimal.
For those of us who lived in the sheltered countryside, it was a
greater challenge. Out there, having a gaijin as a next-door neighbor
is a novelty. You are watched constantly. The initial flattery you
feel from living in a spotlight quickly dissipates. Your job never
ends unless the door is closed, the windows are shut, and you can

sit in your own house alone. Even then, however, the postman may ask why your light was on until 2:00 A.M.

THE PERKS

Many JET participants spend more time being students than teachers during their stay. Living in another country offers the luxury of being able to immerse yourself in its arts and culture, and, in Japan, the treasures are plentiful. Some teachers use the opportunity to study the Japanese language, which also helps them communicate with students in and outside of the classroom; others become proficient in one of the martial arts—judo, karate, or *kendo* (Japanese fencing); many find solace in other art forms, like *ikebana* (flower arranging), *sui-ei* (watercolor drawing), or *shodo* (calligraphy).

Teaching English in the land of the rising sun also means earning the rising yen, which can indeed be profitable. For those drowning in depths of student loans, it offers the capability to pay and still play. That income can also be a ticket to travel to other parts of Japan and Asia. Over the course of two years, I was not only able to see most of Japan, but I also traveled to Hong Kong, Korea, and Thailand.

With passage to and from your posting being paid by the government, JET participants can also travel extensively by asking for the money for the return portion in the form of cash. In this way many of us in the program were able to take the roundabout way home. Some of my friends started out on a slow boat to Korea; others found their way to China, then onto the Trans-Siberian Express and through Europe. Strapped with my ever-growing backpack of dirty laundry and precious souvenirs, I wandered for nearly six months through China, Singapore, Indonesia, New Zealand, Australia, and Fiji. Traveling frugally and living richly, I had no regrets except the loss of a camera and some stunning photos after capsizing my canoe in Tahiti.

A farmer in my village, who is still a dear friend, once told me he was grateful to be around me because I questioned him about his home and everything he took for granted. My curiosity made him stop and wonder why. He liked seeing things through me. In his broken English, he said I gave him a new set of eyes. I think that's what I'd have to say about my two years in Japan: it gave me a different vision of Japan, the world, my home, and myself.

Some Advice from Donna

Bringing Proof: If you plan to look for work, make sure you bring multiple copies of your college diploma or transcript, plus a couple of letters of recommendation from teachers or employers.

Being Able to Get Out: If you go over to Japan without a job, you'll start with a tourist visa. It's important that you have enough cash to pay for the cheapest fare to Hong Kong or Seoul, since you'll need to leave the country to renew your visa or convert it to a working visa.

JET—Picking a Location: If you apply to JET, I recommend that you offer some input on where you'd like to work in Japan. I didn't, because I thought it would jeopardize my chances of being accepted. I later found out that program officials *do* want to know because it facilitates placement. You probably don't want to give an ultimatum, but if it matters to you, be prepared with some opinions.

Shots and Pills: If you plan on traveling in and around Asia, it is a good idea to get fully vaccinated for any possible destinations before you leave home. These will be expensive in Japan and it is not wise to skip them all together. Likewise, if you require a particular medication or have special dietary requirements, stock up before you go.

What to Bring: Make sure you have one decent outfit. As with any job interview, impressions are key, and even teaching English requires at least an initial decorum.

Where to Find Leads: Two good places to look are youth hostels and university notice boards. English newspapers—the Tokyo *Journal* and Japan *Times*, for example—also provide job listings.

A Few Resources to Help You Out

Japanese Exchange and Teaching Program (JET) (Embassy of Japan, 2520 Massachusetts Avenue NW, Washington, D.C. 20008, [202] 939-6700). JET is a program sponsored by the Japanese government to encourage recent graduates to teach English in Japan. In return for one year of teaching, participants are given a salary of approximately $28,000 and a round-trip flight to Japan. Call to receive an application.

Jobs in Japan: The Complete Guide to Living and Working in the Land of Rising Opportunity, by John Wharton (Denver: Global Press, 1988). Lists over four hundred English schools that may hire Americans. It also provides advice on traveling and living in Japan.

International Education Services (IES) (Shin-Taiso Building, 10-7 Dogen-zaka 2-chome, Shibuya-ku, Tokyo, 150 Japan. Fax: [03] 3463-7089). IES is a private program that recruits recent graduates to teach English to business professionals and students. Graduates who join IES are given a work visa, a guaranteed salary, and assistance finding housing in Japan.

International Schools Internship Program (ISIP) (P.O. Box 103, West Bridgewater, Mass. 02379, [508] 580-1880. Fax: [508] 580-2992). ISIP is a program designed for recent graduates interested in teaching Americans and other English-speaking expatriates in private international schools. Participants serve as teacher's aides, tutors, substitute teachers, and coaches in exchange for housing, round-trip transportation, medical insurance, and a monthly living stipend. ISIP works with schools around the world, offering positions almost everywhere, from Bolivia to Bangladesh and Italy to Indonesia.

Circling
the Globe

Margot Weiss

Some people who plunge down a career path immediately after college become caught up in the day-to-day challenges of the working world and lose focus of the larger picture. That's the way Margot was until she decided to take a lap around the globe. She hasn't looked back since.

In the last year, I have fought over a banana with a monkey, fed a kangaroo a Mars bar, and come face-to-face with brumbies—wild horses—in their native Australian bush. I've walked on lava so new that the soles of my boots became gummy from the heat, hiked on a glacier, and trekked in the Himalayas.

Before all this, I led an incredibly normal existence. I graduated from college with a degree in English literature and went straight into a training program at a large publishing company in New York. The closest I got to a foreign country was a subway ride to Chinatown. I felt as though my life would always consist of working, commuting, and longing for weekends and vacations.

So when my friend Richard told me one day, idly, that he was planning a trip around the world, I barely listened. His plans were fantastic, outlandish, and had absolutely nothing to do with my reality. "That sounds great," I said with all the sincerity of a second-place finisher congratulating the winner. "Wish I could do something like that."

To my surprise, Richard said, "You could come with me."

"Me? Travel around the world?" I laughed. "With a job and a two-year lease? No way." But maybe because the day was warm and we were outside in the park, or perhaps because, just for a moment, I wanted to forget all my responsibilities, Richard and I spent hours talking about the countries "we" could visit. He planned to buy something called a round-the-world ticket for about $2,000, which allowed you to fly around the globe, stopping at any ten cities, provided you always flew in the same direction. The ticket was good for a year.

At the end of the afternoon, he asked me again if I would come. "I'll think about it," I told him, knowing it was impossible.

GOING?? GOING? GONE!

I spent the next four months thinking about it. I shared my dilemma with my family and friends and begged them constantly for advice: "What should I do?" "I know you can't *tell* me, but what do you *think* I should do?" "Would *you* go?"

Everyone told me to go, but they could find hundreds of reasons not to go themselves.

I began to make what I told myself were just-in-case preparations. I visited the doctor and the dentist, renewed my passport, and got all of my immunization shots. I found a tentative subletter, took travel books out of the library, and visited foreign embassies to ask for maps, brochures, and visas. But the one thing I would not do— the one thing I needed to do—was buy a ticket.

And then one day Richard called me and told me in a no-nonsense kind of way that he was going to buy his ticket that day and did I want one as well? I took a deep breath, crossed my fingers, and said yes.

One month later I was in Fiji, with New Zealand, Australia, Hong Kong, Thailand, Burma, Nepal, and India still to come.

International I.D.

Name LIKE A COMPLETE UNKNOWN

Address NO DIRECTION HOME

HT 5'7" WT 130 DOB 073172

Nationality: **BACKPACKER**

CRAZY, LAZY, OR NONE OF THE ABOVE?

My trip was official. I had crossed the international date line and had a stamp in my passport. Work, Manhattan, my friends, and family bordered an ocean so far away they were literally in the past. The new landscapes enthralled me, yet my times for reflection—journal writing, reading letters from home—were weighed with nagging fears. Would I get so hooked on traveling that I would fall off my career track permanently? Was I being more self-indulgent than productive?

When we landed on one of the tiny tourist islands in Fiji, a realization hit me like a thump on the head: *I'm not the only one doing this. I'm not crazy. Or lazy.* The island was crowded with other travelers. They too carried bags on their backs that, like the shells of turtles, comprised "home." Suddenly I had a new identity: backpacker.

The backpackers I met were eighteen-year-old Brits on preuniversity tours and retirees who could have been their parents. There were travel agents and architects, hair cutters and grocery store managers, bankers and bums. They were all ages, all levels of experience and income. They were Europeans and Australians and Canadians and, rarely, Americans. During long, warm, beer-drenched evenings, we traded backgrounds, plans, and adventures.

From our conversations I learned not just why they traveled but how they traveled. I had known about study years abroad, educational tours, business trips, and vacations. But these were people who traveled not to get somewhere but to *be* somewhere, taking from one to five years to see as much of the world as they could because they knew it was an experience as self-broadening as time spent at a university could be and more intrinsically valuable than the money pocketed from a nine-to-five office job. I began to think of an extensive trip as simply something one does, as valid as a profession. Quite a shock to my insular, American view.

FINDING A RHYTHM

My trip wasn't an easy one. In the space of five months, I visited eight countries, while most of the people I encountered had allotted twice as long for half as much. The intense schedule gave me an overview of many countries but left so much undiscovered. Rather than knowing a few countries well, I can now say with authority which countries I would like to return to for a longer period of time in the future.

I packed as many experiences as I could into every country, often spending just one or two days in a place and then moving on. By June, three months into the trip, the strange rhythm had begun to feel normal. The weight of my pack seemed comfortable. Almost forgotten was the day I'd first strapped it on and pitched butt-first into my living room couch. I could go up to people casually and ask them where they were from or where they were going, without feeling as though I was using a pickup line. I gave passing nostalgic thought only to luxuries like a private bed and bathroom, wearing a dress, or eating sushi. Then I would hurry on to my next adventure.

In New Zealand I weathered a four-day trek in the icy rain. In Australia I learned to sail and decided a tattoo would be a good, portable souvenir. In Thailand I fended off malaria-ridden mosquitos the size of small helicopters and sloshed my way through a street flooded knee-high with monsoon rain. But despite my increased assurance, I knew that the biggest challenge of my trip was still to come.

INDIA

When we landed in Bombay and drove through the steamy heat past slums crowded with naked, dusty children, I felt far more unsettled and afraid than I had yet. I was terrified of getting sick, terrified of the sheer difficulty of traveling, but I was even more afraid of being overwhelmed by India and having to cut my trip short. Talking to people who had traveled in India, I had heard two distinct reactions to the country. Some people loved it, reveling in the colorful history, the pervasive religions and cultures, the sheer exoticness of the land, the people, the food. Others had left after an agonizing few weeks and divulged stories of unendurable travel and accommodations and dysentery-induced hospital stays.

The effect on me was dual and immense. Simply because India was so terribly difficult and unpleasant at times, so outstandingly exotic at others, my experiences there are impossible to encapsulate. More than a year after my trip, it's the only country I still dream about—dreams replete with the deafening roar of the streets, the smell of burning cow manure used for fuel, the milky, densely smokey taste of the tea. There were days in India when I wished I'd never gone and swore never to return, but now I find it difficult to imagine the narrowness of my life not knowing a little bit about this world that exists simultaneously with, and yet so differently from, ours. It was a tough four weeks before I began to get a grip on the country and, more important, before it began to get a grip on me.

PUSHKAR, RAJASTHAN

I arrived in Pushkar near the end of July, and as I often did on my first day in a new town, I took off to explore on foot. After wandering through the Main Bazaar, browsing, I eventually ended up at the foot of a high temple with a great number of devout Hindus lining up outside to worship. Why not? I said to myself. When will I ever again have a chance to learn about Hinduism in one of the holiest cities in the world?

I bought some rose petals and some stuff that looked like puffed rice and left my sandals with a man who charged me the tourist price, five rupees (fifteen cents). Barefoot, I climbed the high stone steps to the temple and watched everyone in front of me carefully. When I reached the shrine, I knelt and gave the men inside my puffed rice and rose petals and received some in return, as well as a thimbleful of water, which I poured on my head.

Behind the temple, some fellow worshipers gave me some of their rice and petals in exchange for mine. Suddenly I was circled by about twenty-five people, all of whom wanted some of my puffed rice. I felt like a sideshow surrounded by these curious faces and lilting voices—"Thank you, madam!" or "*Mamaste!*" ("May the blessings of God be with you"). I poured rice into every outstretched hand. Many people spoke to me, and I tried to imbue my smiles and clumsy attempts to repeat what they had said with some kind of meaning.

A man brought his elderly parents forward and asked to introduce them to me. When they saw me, they touched their foreheads as a mark of respect, and I repeated the gesture. The mother clasped her arm around my shoulders with a broad smile. With the others surrounding both of us now, she proceeded to march me down the temple stairs and back through the street, all the while shouting in Hindi to bystanders, who looked on with surprise, amusement, and confusion.

A man on the street stopped me briefly. "Do you know what she's saying?" I shook my head. He translated, "She's from my country! This woman is from my country!"

I was pulled aside many times and asked to meet children and shake hands with wives (who, not speaking English, were prompted by their husbands to say, "Thank you, madam"). A younger woman began to hold my hand and some more women draped my brazenly exposed head and shoulders in a large scarf. We reached my hotel quickly, but in that short journey, I had seen a new part of India that had touched me deeply.

Unfortunately, just as I was learning to feel my way in India, it was almost time to leave. My regrets at departing, though, were completely overshadowed by my physical and mental exhaustion. In addition to recovering from dysentery, I was absolutely over- whelmed by the impressions I'd accumulated over five months, and I longed to sit and digest my experiences. I'd begun to fantasize about the smell of new grass, a cool breeze, a fresh tomato, any food that wasn't Indian. I longed for the relative sanity, peace, and cleanliness of the animal- and rickshaw-free Manhattan streets. My dreams of taking a shower, of drinking pure, clean water straight from the tap, and changing into something I hadn't worn for the past five months brought me so much pleasure they bordered on the erotic.

It was time to go home.

———————

Whatever you do, don't say to yourself that you can't travel. You can. And it's important. Work for half a year to save some money and take off. And if you're still torn, here's one of the best pieces of advice I received while trying to reach my own decision: what are you going to remember in forty years, your office job or a trip around the world?

Now, little more than a year later, I remember the deep rumbling of a Himalayan avalanche, the colorful parrot fish eating out of my hand, and the primitive, terrifying beauty of a spray of molten lava hitting the ocean.

But I'll be damned if I can remember how to unjam that copy machine.

In a way, my trip hasn't ended yet. Now I'm living in Germany with a friend I met in Australia. I'm teaching English and learning a new language. There's a world of difference between my life now and my original career plan, but there's also a world of difference between the person who hesitated about buying an airplane ticket and the person reflecting now on that hesitation. A wonderful, beautiful, fascinating world.

I know. I'm lucky enough to have seen some of it.

Some Advice from Margot

Airplane Tickets: Check the travel section of one of the larger newspapers for round-the-world or circle pacific tickets. Make sure to check out the company. Try to buy a flexible ticket in case your plans change midtrip.

Guide Books: Lonely Planet guidebooks are wonderful—as informative, accurate, and hip as publishing lead times allow.

Health: As you're making your plans, call the Centers for Disease Control in North Carolina ([404] 639-2572) and listen to their prerecorded messages for the most up-to-date information available on infectious diseases, prevention, and treatment around the world. For immunizations, your local board of health should be able to tell you where to go.

Planning: You don't have to plan as much as you think you do. Somehow things seem to work out. Someone will always have a hostel to recommend, a route to take, a sight to see, and a place to eat. Don't panic.

Unpredictability: If you do have a plan or a schedule, definitely pencil in flexibility. You may meet a potential friend and travel together; a city might need two weeks instead of one; or an avalanche may delay your bus for hours. It's always wise to overbudget your time. Traveling is harder and slower than drawing lines on a map.

A Few Resources to Help You Out

Lonely Planet Publications (P.O. Box 2001A, Berkeley, Calif. 94702). Lonely Planet guidebooks, aptly called travel survival kits, are ideal for low-budget travelers. Each region-specific book offers practical information on where to go, what to eat, and where to stay, and is combined with well-researched historical material and interesting anecdotal tidbits. Definitely worth the extra weight in your pack.

The Berkeley Guides: The Budget Traveler's Handbook (New York: Random House). Another excellent series of econo-travel guidebooks, researched and written by Berkeley students.

Insider's Guide to Air Courier Bargains: How to Travel World-Wide for Next to Nothing, by Kelly Monaghan (New York: Intrepid Traveler, 1994). For graduates who can travel light and leave on short notice, being a courier is a great way to get to faraway lands for next to nothing. This book gives you the inside scoop on how to do it.

A Journey of One's Own: Uncommon Advice for the Independent Woman Traveler, by Thalia Zepatos (Portland, Oreg.: Eighth Mountain Press, 1992). A pleasing combination of practical advice and travel anecdotes. The author offers sound thoughts on important issues such as sexual harassment, safety, and health, along with inspiring ideas on how to live out a fulfilling solo travel adventure.

Travelers' Health: How to Stay Healthy All Over the World, by Richard Dawood, M.D. (New York: Random House, 1994). A comprehensive guide of what not to catch and how to treat it if you do.

Finding
Your Bliss

Dan Cavicchio

As Dan discovered, no one can tell you what to do after college except you. Which is why this enlightened beginning is a perfect ending to this book.

A Colorado cowboy named Doyle once taught me a good lesson about life. Doyle was about seventy years old when I met him. He wore a genuine Stetson hat, faded blue jeans, and big leather boots. Even though Doyle looked like something right out of the old West, he was actually more of a modern-day cowboy—he spent his time with machines, not cattle. Every day Doyle woke up at 4:00 A.M. and went off to work at a local farm. His job was to run a hay baler, a tractorlike machine that cuts and binds grass.

If I remember right, Doyle worked six days a week. He worked hard, too. His day ran from sunrise until six o'clock at night. I don't even know if he took time off for lunch. I had heard all about Doyle and his job before I even met him, and all I could think was, Poor guy. I mean, running a hay baler was pretty hard work. How much fun could a person have driving a machine up and down a field? And six days a week? His job seemed so boring to me. There were no challenges for him, no creativity.

When I finally met Doyle, there was some sympathy in my eyes. But the funny thing was, there was a whole lot more sympathy in *his* eyes.

"I heard about you," he said, shaking my hand.

"About me?"

"Yeah," he said. "I just want to tell you to hang on in there. I know it's hard."

I didn't understand what he meant. "What's hard?"

"College," he said. "I heard you're in college."

"Well, yes," I said. "I am."

He shook his head. "It must be awful. I've heard lots of stories."

"Stories?"

"Sure. I've heard about all those books you have to read. And all that writing. I hear you have to stay up all night writing sometimes." He whistled. "It must be tough."

It took me a second to answer. "Well, sure," I said. "There is a lot of that, but, you know, it's actually kind of fun."

"Fun?" he said. "I can't imagine it. I'd be miserable sitting there with all those books."

"But it's actually not that bad. . . ."

"I'd hate it. Now me, on the other hand, I've got the best job there is. Just look at that sun. I get to see it rise every morning and set every night. And there just isn't a better spot on the earth than this farm. I can't tell you how lucky I am."

"Really?"

"It's the best. So, like I said, just hang on in there. Someday you'll be out of college, and you can come back here and work like this. Just hang on in there."

And that was my meeting with Doyle.

Now, before I met Doyle, I had a pretty firm idea about careers. I knew what was at the top and bottom of the career list and figured everyone else felt the same way. It seemed pretty clear to me. The top job was something well paid on Wall Street, something with lots of perks. Also high on the list were the service-to-society jobs— teaching or laboratory research. Then there was that awful segment at the bottom: labor. That was by far the worst.

But then here was Doyle, running his hay baler up and down the fields and loving every minute of it. This just didn't compute. I mean, Doyle wasn't simply resigned to his job—he lived for it. He woke up early every morning out of sheer excitement for the job. The farm manager later told me that he couldn't find enough hay-baling work for Doyle to do, the man loved it so much.

By the time I got back to college several weeks later, my ideas about careers had begun to un-gel. Doyle, I realized, wasn't on that farm by chance, nor was he there because his job was remarkably glamorous. Doyle was there because he loved to drive a hay baler. And so I was stuck with the questions: What do I love to do? Do I really love the idea of working on Wall Street? No, actually, I didn't. Wall Street just seemed so glitzy. Did I love the idea of being in a classroom or in a lab, doing research? No, not particularly—it's just that everyone else was talking about that sort of thing. How about running a hay baler? No, that was for Doyle alone.

My time in college passed and I kept asking the question: What in the world do I love to do? The truth was that I had always been such a competitor. I knew where the brass rings were in life and I rode around until I finally grabbed at them. That, if anything, was what I was good at. But meeting Doyle made me realize that there are no brass rings, at least not in the way I thought. Not everyone in the world wanted to work in finance and not everyone hated the thought of farm labor. The whole game began to blur.

I finally took a look around me at the people who, like Doyle, seemed to be doing what they loved. And what I found were some very strange things. Here was a man running a coffee shop that doubled as a nonprofit company. Over there was a geographer who spent his time studying world hunger. Here was a woman running a "Center for Sound Healing." And there was a doctor lecturing on Indian philosophy. They were very strange occupations, all of them. But all of these people seemed extraordinarily fulfilled. Like Doyle, they were filling a function unique to them, a function they must have found somewhere within. I mean, how else do you establish a Center for Sound Healing? Certainly not because everyone else is doing it.

After struggling a bit, I decided to try to be like them. I would look for what I loved and spend my time doing it. When I made the decision, it was almost summer. I was living in Providence, Rhode Island, at the time, in a tiny old house built during the colonial era. I had a little money in the bank and I was ready to begin. For three months there would be no jobs waiting tables, no schoolwork, and no thoughts about long-term plans. I'd simply try to do what I loved.

During the first week of June, I planted a garden. There was a little rectangle of dirt in our front yard and it seemed like it wanted attention. I cleaned the garbage and glass out of the dirt. I added some richer-looking soil. Then I planted an assortment of zucchini and pumpkin plants, plus some flowers. When the garden was done, I turned to the house.

The walls of my house were crumbling, so I patched them up with some spackle. I negotiated with my landlord to buy two gallons of paint and I went to work on that, too. Spackle, scrape, paint. Spackle, scrape, paint. It went on like this for weeks. In the past, I had never liked home-improvement work. But for some reason, it's what I felt like doing.

After a few weeks spent working on the house, a new desire hit me. I wanted to write. I began to work on a short essay and had a good time doing it. I actually made a little money from it when it was published in my college alumni magazine. I spent a lot of time in cafés. I did some volunteer work. I freelanced as a graphic designer. Even the garden did pretty well, yielding a good four or five zucchinis by the end. And the funny thing is, I always had enough money. I don't know how it all worked out, but it did.

Joseph Campbell, the scholar of mythology, is known for the famous tag line "Follow your bliss." "Follow your joy," he said, "and you'll end up in the right place." And he lived it. When he was thirty, Campbell retired to a cabin in the woods to "read the classics." Another time he spent a few years deciphering James Joyce's *Finnegan's Wake*. He hung out with John Steinbeck, free-lanced as a jazz musician, and taught classes at Sarah Lawrence

College. All because he was following his heart. It takes a lot of courage, but Campbell showed that it could be done.

And that, I guess, is where I am today. I'm trying my best to follow my heart. It's not always easy, but things brighten up when I give myself room to do what I want. Sometimes it's writing. Other times it's coffee with a friend. Often it's just sitting around trying to clear out my mind. The hardest part so far has been ignoring all the voices that say, Follow your bliss? It can't be done.

Whenever I begin to worry, though, I just think of old Doyle. He's still there on his hay-baling machine, riding up and down the Colorado fields. Doyle's following his heart. He's respecting his dreams. He's doing what he loves in life, and I hope to follow his lead.

So ... What *did* you do after college?

If you're reading this book, you may not have an answer to this question yet. But when you do, we'd love to hear about it. The people who wrote the essays in this book were recent graduates who wanted to share a little about what they discovered after college. Their stories cover some of the possibilities, but there are so many other options. And we'd love to include them in the next edition of this book. So if you enjoy writing, why not tell us about *your* experiences? We want to know what it's like to start your own business, be an assistant buyer in high fashion, walk the Appalachian trail, work as a bicycle messenger, and just about everything else. Also, we'd welcome any tips, advice, or resources you may come across along the way. If you've found a great book about working in the music industry, have a hot tip on how to find a job teaching English abroad, or know of a useful organization for freelance writers, drop us a line. Or if you're off traveling the world, send us a postcard. We want to know what it's like out there!

Write to:
So ... What *Are* You Doing After College?
P.O. Box 640243
San Francisco, CA 94164